The Virgin Birth of J

By

G.H. Box

CHAPTER I. INTRODUCTORY

Have the Gospel narratives of the Nativity, in their canonical form, been influenced by pagan conceptions? No apology is needed for asking once more and endeavoring to answer this question in view of the critical controversy that has within recent years invaded not only our scholastic, but also popular theological literature. The questions in debate have, of course, long ceased to be of merely academic interest, and involve issues of grave practical importance to Christians generally. With the theological question involved, however, it is not the purpose of the present volume to deal at any length. The writer s primary aim is to discuss, in as objective a manner as he can, the alleged influence of pagan ideas on the Nativity-Narratives of the First and Third Gospels, and the questions that arise therefrom.

According to the latest exponents of one branch of the critical school there is not the faintest shadow of doubt as to what the true answer to our question is. What the Christian Church has always regarded as the central fact of the narratives in question the Virgin Birth is without hesitation assigned in these quarters to a purely pagan origin. Thus, according to Usener, "for the whole birth and childhood story of Mt. (Matthew) in its every detail it is possible to trace a pagan sub-stratum. It must have arisen in Gentile-Christian circles, probably in those of the province of Asia, and then was to some extent legitimated by its narrator in accordance with the tendency manifested through out the whole of the First Gospel by citation of prophetic words in its support." With this conclusion, also, Schmiedel agrees. According to him, "the origin of the idea of a virgin birth is to be sought in Gentile-Christian circles."

Soltau's estimate, though more guarded, is also in substantial agreement with the foregoing: "May we not suppose," he says, "that the Virgin Birth of Jesus had a similar (heathen) origin (to that of the episodes of the angels Song of Praise, Luke ii. 8, and of the magi)?"

In view of the pronouncedly Jewish-Christian character of the Nativity-Narratives of the Gospels such conclusions at first sight certainly seem to savor of paradox. How can such an essentially pagan idea have found entrance into Jewish-Christian circles? In order to elucidate this question, it will be necessary to discuss the character of the narratives afresh. If their Palestinian or semi-Palestinian origin can be sustained, the hypo thesis of direct pagan influence must be ruled out, as Soltau, indeed, admits. For the purposes of this discussion, it will be convenient to deal with the narrative of the First Gospel first, since it is here, according to Usener, that pagan influence is pronounced throughout. Moreover, it will readily be conceded that Mt. account, whatever be its origin, is almost (if not wholly) independent of that of Luke.

A cursory examination of the Gospel-narratives is sufficient to reveal certain apparent inconsistencies of statement and implication regarding the parentage of Jesus. He is popularly regarded and spoken of as the son of Joseph (cf. Matthew xiii. 55, "Is not this the carpenter's son?"; Luke iv. 23; John i. 45, vi. 42; and even in the Nativity-Narrative of the Third Gospel, Mary and Joseph are several times referred to as "his parents." (Luke ii. 27, 41, 43), while once the mother of Jesus herself is made to say: "Thy father (i.e., Joseph) and I sought thee sorrowing" (ii. 48). It is quite clear that Jesus was popularly looked upon by His contemporaries as Joseph's son by natural generation. On the other hand, both the First and the Third Gospels contain special sections dealing with the circumstances of the birth of Jesus in detail, and, though obviously independent, the two traditions embodied in the Nativity-Narratives agree in stating unequivocally that Jesus was born of a virgin-mother without the intervention of a human father (Matthew i. 18; Luke i. 34, 35).

No real inconsistency is, however, necessarily involved in the narratives as they stand. The secret of Jesus birth may have been for long jealously guarded within the narrow circle of persons among whom it was originally known. It apparently formed no part of the early Apostolic teaching and preaching, and was not included in the common form of the Synoptic Gospel-Tradition (note that the Second Gospel begins with the Baptism). In preserving, therefore, the popular references to Jesus as Joseph s son, the First and Third Gospels conform to psychological and historic truth. In one part of the narrative, popular opinion is accurately reflected and expressed; in the other, knowledge of a special character, derived from private sources.

That no inconsistency was felt to exist in this double use of description appears from the fact that it occurs even in the Apocryphal Gospels, where the virginity of the mother of Jesus is often insisted upon with unnecessary stress. Thus in the Gospel of pseudo-Matthew (ch. xxvii.) the following, e.g., occurs: "And some went away to the chief priests, and to the chiefs of the Pharisees, and told them that Jesus the son of Joseph had done great signs," etc. A few pages further on (ch. xxx.), Jesus is made to say: "But I am an alien in your courts, because I have no carnal parent."

On the other hand, if such references as those cited above from the Gospels had exhibited a mechanical consistency in describing Jesus as the son of Mary (to the entire exclusion of

Joseph), the representation would justly have been impugned as violating the canons of historical and psychological truth.

In social life and as a member of the Jewish nation, Jesus, during His earthly life, would necessarily be regarded as Joseph s son. As Dalman has pointed out: "If no other fatherhood was alleged, then the child must have been regarded as bestowed by God upon the house of Joseph;" and while Joseph was alive, Mary and her son were undoubtedly under his legal protection. This consideration will help to explain the fact that both genealogies trace the Davidic descent of Jesus through Joseph (not through Mary). On any view, Jesus belonged to the family of Joseph; and if any formal and official birth-register ever had an independent existence in the Temple or elsewhere, Jesus would naturally appear therein as Joseph s son.

It will be necessary to refer to some of these points at greater length in the pages that follow. In the succeeding chapters it is proposed to discuss the birth-narratives of the First and Third Gospels (chapters ii.-v.), the Birth and Childhood of Jesus in the Apocryphal Gospels (ch. vi.),the evidence of the other New Testament writings and the earliest Christian tradition (outside the Gospels) (ch. vii.), and the alleged parallels from heathen sources (ch. viii.). In a final chapter (ix.), an attempt will be made to appraise the results that have been reached.

CHAPTER II.THE NARRATIVE OF ST. MATTHEW (MT.)

I – THE JEWISH CHARACTER OF MATTHEW I AND II

The first impression produced by the perusal of Mt.'s narrative is, undoubtedly, that we have here a genuine product of the Jewish spirit. In spirit, as well as in letter and substance, it reflects the characteristic features of Jewish habits of thought and expression. How strong this impression is and how well founded may be gathered from the remarks of so unprejudiced an observer as Prof. S. Schechter. "The impression," he says, "conveyed to the Rabbinic student by the perusal of the New Testament is in many parts like that gained by reading an old Rabbinic homily. On the very threshold of the New Testament he is confronted by a genealogical table, a feature not uncommon in the later Rabbinical versions of the Old Testament, which are rather fond of providing Biblical heroes with long pedigrees. They are not always accurate, but have, as a rule, some edifying purpose in view. In the second chapter of Matthew the Rabbinic student meets with many features known to him from the Rabbinic narratives about the birth of Abraham; the story of the Magi, in particular, impresses him as a homiletical illustration of Numb. xxiv. 17: "There shall come a Star out of Jacob, which Star the interpretation of the Synagogue referred to the Star of the Messiah."

It is not necessary at this point to insist further on the admittedly Jewish character of the genealogy in the First Gospel. But it is worth recalling here that the representation of the relations between Joseph and Mary in Matt. i. is in strict accordance with Jewish law, according to which a betrothed woman "occupied the same status as a wife," and the child bestowed upon her, if recognized by the father, "must" (to use Dalman's words) "have been regarded as bestowed by God upon the house of Joseph."

Another point that is important in this connexion is the explanation of the name Jesus in v. 21 ("He shall be called Jesus because he shall save," etc.). This involves a play upon words which points to a Hebrew origin (yeshu a yosim a), at any rate, for this particular verse. Without affirming a Hebrew original for the Nativity-Narrative of Mt. as it stands (which is a highly precarious hypothesis), this indication at least serves to suggest that the compiler was writing for readers who were not wholly unacquainted with Hebrew, and who, at any rate, could appreciate the significance of the connexion between the Hebrew words yeshu a (Jesus) and yoshi a (shall save); that is, it may be inferred, he was writing for Hellenistic Jews who were not out of touch with Palestine, and to whom the Hebrew Bible would not be altogether unfamiliar.

But what seems to us to be an even more decisive indication of the influence of Palestine in this narrative, is the elaborate explanation and justification of the name "Nazarene" (Ch. ii. 22, 23), as applied to Our Lord. In this way the compiler turns the edge of the reproach leveled at the Christian Messiah in the characteristically Palestinian-Jewish designation of Jesus as "The Nazarene".

It may be concluded, then, that the whole narrative embodied in the first two chapters of the First Gospel is thoroughly Jewish in form and general conception, and that, while Hellenistic coloring is unmistakably present in the story, it shows decisive indications of the influence of Palestine, and is, in fact, addressed to a circle of Hellenistic Jews who were under Palestinian influence. A word must now be said about the integrity of the narrative, and its historical character and significance.

II. THE NATIVITY-NARRATIVE AN INTEGRAL PART
OF THE FIRST GOSPEL

Does the Nativity-Narrative (Mt. i.-ii.) form an integral part of the First Gospel as it left the compilers hands? According to some scholars, the answer to this question must be a decided negative. Thus, after discussing the genealogy and arguing for the originality of the reading of the Sinaitic Syriac Palimpsest in i. 16 (Joseph begat Jesus who is called the Christ), concludes that the following narrative (i. 18-ii. 23) formed no part of the original Matthew, which began the history at iii., at the point where the narrative of the Second Gospel commences; the only difference between the two Evangels being that the original form of the First Gospel had prefixed to it the Birth-Register embodied in Mt. i. 1-17.

To us, this conclusion seems to be wholly irreconcilable with the data afforded by the genealogy itself. The remarkable additions in vv. 3, 5, and 6 b. of the names of certain women are clearly out of place in a formal genealogy of Joseph, unless they are dictated by some apologetic purpose. They are doubtless intended, as Mr. (now Archdeacon) Willoughby C. Allen has pointed out, "to prepare the mind of his (the evangelists) readers for the following narrative as in some sort foreshadowing the overruling of circumstances by the Divine Providence in the case of the Virgin Mary."

From the genealogy itself it may, therefore, be inferred (whatever be the true text of i. 16) that the subsequent narrative is its proper sequel; and from the special didactic character of the genealogy (which fundamentally dominates its structure, and so entirely accords with the distinctive peculiarities of the Gospel as a whole) it may safely be inferred that both the birth-register and its sequel are the work of the compiler of the First Gospel.

III. THE GENERAL CHARACTER AND HISTORICAL
SIGNIFICANCE OF ST. MATTHEW'S NATIVITY-NARRATIVE

What, then, is the general character and historical significance of St. Matthew's narration (Mt. i. and ii.)? To us it seems to exhibit in a degree that can hardly be paralleled elsewhere in the New Testament the characteristic features of Jewish Midrash or Haggada. 1 It sets forth certain facts and beliefs in a fanciful and imaginative setting, specially calculated to appeal to Jews. The justification for this procedure lies in the peculiar character and idiosyncrasy of the readers to whom it is addressed. The same tendency can be seen at work all through the First Gospel, and even elsewhere in the New Testament (e.g., in St. Paul 2), though in a far less pronounced form. The task that confronts the critical student is to disentangle the facts and beliefs the fundamental ground factors on which the narration is built from their decorative embroidery.

What, then, are these fundamental data?

(a) The Genealogy (i. 1-17)

The artificial and Midrashic character of the genealogy is obvious and admitted. It is dominated by a didactic purpose. This is clearly shown in its structure (3 x 14 generations), in the insertion of "the King" in which, to borrow Mr. Allen's words, "seems clearly to show that the compiler wishes to emphasize the acquisition of royal power in David, its loss at the captivity, its recovery in the Messiah. It is hardly necessary to prove (he goes on to say) that else where in the Gospel the Kingship of Christ is brought into relief;" and also in the additions of the names of certain women, already referred to.

The explanation of the three fourteens put forward long ago by seems to us to be quite possible. He suggests that it is based upon the numerical value of the Hebrew letters which make up the name David the threefold repetition being due to the fact that the name is made up of three letters.

By this means, the genealogy was invested with the character of a sort of numeral acrostic on the name David (in). However artificial such a procedure may seem to us, it is thoroughly Jewish, and could easily be illustrated in other ways. Thus, a Rabbinical dictum runs: The Book of Chronicles (which, it should be remembered, was the source and fount for genealogical lists par excellence) was only given for the sake of being "interpreted," or, as we might render the Hebrew term (lidrdsh), "for Midrashic purposes" (i.e., for the moral and edifying lessons that may be deduced therefrom). It is worth noting also that its ascending structure (Abraham begat Isaac; and Isaac begat Jacob, etc.) is exactly similar to that of the little genealogy of David that closes the Book of Ruth, which may also have been appended for apologetic purposes.

The fundamental fact which underlies the genealogy of the First Gospel, and to which it bears witness, is the Davidic descent of the family of Joseph to which Jesus belonged. Its artificial form merely serves to disguise a genuine family tradition, which may have been embodied in a real birth-register. May it not be a sort of Midrashic commentary, in genealogical terms, on the real genealogy which is more correctly preserved in the Third Gospel?

To us it also seems probable that, in making the remarkable additions of the names of the women in vv. 3, 5, and 6 b, the compiler intended to anticipate (or meet) Jewish calumnies regarding Jesus birth, which were afterwards amplified in so nauseous a fashion in later Jewish literature, and which find their explanation in a distortion of the Christian version of the Virgin Birth. The compiler implicitly, and by anticipation, rebuts this reproach by throwing it back upon the Royal House of Judah.

As has already been pointed out, some scholars hold that the genealogy set forth in Matt. i. 1-17, originally existed in an independent form, and was taken over by the compiler of the First Gospel, who may have added the names of the women in vv. 3, 5, and 6 b.; and in this form it plainly stated that Joseph begat Jesus (v. 17). But against this view is the artificial character of the genealogy already referred to above. It can hardly be regarded as in any sense an actual birth-register. Its real purpose is not historical, but didactic. It is merely an embodiment in genealogical form a form specially calculated to appeal to Jewish readers of the idea that Jesus belonged, through His relation to Joseph, to the royal family of David. Such a purpose exactly accords with the whole presentation of Mt. There is therefore no sufficient reason to regard it as anything else than the work of Mt. Even if the reading Joseph begat Jesus be correct, it need not imply a belief in the natural generation of Jesus. It obviously does not do so, if the writer of vv. 18-25 also composed the genealogy itself. For he immediately proceeds, as if to correct any possible misapprehension: Now, as a matter of fact, the birth of Christ was in this wise (v. 18). It is often forgotten that a formal genealogy makes no provision for such an unique event as a virgin birth. The compiler is endeavoring to express two things which he regarded as facts: (1) Jesus belonged to the royal family of Judah; (2) Jesus is virgin-born. The fact that Jesus and His mother were taken under Joseph s protection, and thus became members of his family, was sufficient to establish the relationship, for all legal and ordinary purposes, of "father and son" between Joseph and Jesus. This fact is expressed, in genealogical language by the terms (if the reading be correct): Joseph begat Jesus.

(b) The Birth-Narrative (i. 18-25)

In the narrative that follows (i. 18-25) we are confronted by similar phenomena the underlying fact accompanied by explanation. The fact assumed and explicitly stated is the Virgin Birth, which is supported (in the compiler s characteristic manner) by a citation from Scripture, viz., the LXX. Version of Isa. vii. 14.

Now, it is generally agreed that the narrative cannot have been suggested by the citation. It is certainly remarkable that Isa. vii. 14, is the only passage in the LXX. (with one exception, viz., Gen. xxiv. 43), where the Hebrew word "alma," which means a young woman of marriageable age, is rendered Trapdevos; in the over whelming majority of instances irapoevos corresponds to the proper Hebrew equivalent behold. Moreover, of any Messianic application among the Jews of these words concerning the Virgin's Son, there is not elsewhere, we are assured on the high authority of Prof. Dalman, even a "trace." Consequently, we are justified in the conclusion that the narrative was not suggested by the citation, but the citation by the assumed fact of the narrative. Another point brought out and emphasized in the quotation is the significance of the term Immanuel. Jesus is represented as realizing in Himself the prophetic word about Immanuel, not because He bore Immanuers name, but because in His person the full significance of the name "God with us" had become a fact. The name according to M. Halevy, is interpreted not metaphorically, but literally as meaning that God had appeared among men in the person of Jesus; in other words, that Jesus is God Incarnate. This representation is also reinforced by the explanation of the personal name Jesus as meaning one who saves His people from their sins, a function reserved in the Old Testament for God alone, which could be exercised by no merely human being.

The narrative of Mt., therefore, though it moves, to use M. Halevy's words, "dans une atmosphere phariseenne," must on this view be regarded as dominated by an advanced Christology.

We believe, however, that this view is not widely shared by Christian critical scholars. Thus, the writer of the article on "The Virgin Birth" in the American Journal of Theology already referred to (for July, 1902) explains the meaning of the birth story in Matthew as follows: "Matthew's thought seems to be," he says, "that the wonder-working spirit of God exclusive of human agency, caused Mary to conceive; that by reason of this fact, she was innocent of any wrong such as that the suspicion of which had troubled Joseph; and that at the same time such a birth, being in accord with the Immanuel-prophecy, marked the child to be born as the Messiah, the Savior of His people, as the one spoken of in Isaiah, chapters vii. and viii., to be the deliverer of his nation in the impending war. Thus the application of the prophetic and symbolic expression Immanuel was not for the purpose of designating the nature of the child, but rather his work, which was to be national and messianic. The result of the nation s sins was always the withdrawal of God; but the Messiah would lead them in righteousness and save them from that abandoning by God which was at the same time the result of their sins and the cause of their impotence and subjection. The term Immanuel, then, is the prophetic and symbolic designation for Savior."

According to this view, the compiler's main concern is to explain something which was obviously regarded as a fact within the Christian circle to which he belonged, but which was a source of reproach to the Jewish circles outside, whose objections he constantly had in mind when composing his Gospel. Such a birth as that described, he contends, actually fulfils the prophetic word about Messiah's birth; beyond this he does not go. In other words, his governing purpose is not theological or speculative, but apologetic and practical.

(c) The Episodes in Chapter ii

The form of the narrative embodied in chapter ii exhibits much the same characteristics as the preceding. Its Midrashic character is evident throughout, and it is governed by an apologetic purpose. But the dominant facts and beliefs do not show so obviously on the surface. Throughout, the evangelistic writer, according to Zahn, is drawing an elaborate parallel between Israel's national history and the personal history of the Christian Messiah. Just as the genealogy is designed to show that the birth of the Messianic King forms the climax of Israel's history, so here, especially in the episode of the Flight into and Return from Egypt, the writer intends Israel to draw a parallel between the history of its own national youth and the episodes of the early years of Jesus. The fatherly, relationship that had been metaphorically ascribed; to Jahveh as regards Israel (e.g., Deut. xxxii. 13: Of the Rock that begat thee thou art unmindful, and hast forgotten God that gave thee birth) is, the Evangelist implies, fulfilled in a real and literal sense in Jesus; who, though belonging to the family of David, and, therefore, David s son, was the Son of God, without the intervention of a human father, by the power of the Holy Ghost. Consequently, the citation from Hosea xi (Out of Egypt have I called my son), which in its original context can have only a national reference, is, from the Evangelist's standpoint, a perfectly consistent proceeding. The use of Scriptural citations, throughout, is, indeed, remarkable. The writer regards the prophetic words as charged with a wealth of hitherto unexhausted meaning, which, in the light of Jesus life-history, have acquired a new or widely extended significance. He constantly introduces such citations with the striking formula "that it might be fulfilled;" and when this is modified the alteration is probably intentional.

The narratives, then, have a basis in fact, or what is assumed to be or regarded as fact. But in form they have often been assimilated to earlier models and display unmistakable Midrashic features. Thus, the form in which the episode of the Return from Egypt is narrated in vv. 20 and 21 is clearly modeled upon the LXX of Exodus iv. 19, 20 (the return of Moses from Midian to Egypt).

And this, perhaps, affords the true key for interpreting the apologetic significance of the rest of the narrative. The Evangelist intends to suggest a likeness between the divinely guided career of Moses, the instrument of Israel's redemption from Egypt, and the Messianic Redeemer who saves His people from their sins the type, of course, being far transcended by the antitype.

Thus, the Story of the Magi, with its astrological features, has a very striking parallel in the Midrash Rabba to Exodus in the section which deals with the birth of Moses. In the passage in question, we are told that Pharaoh s astrologers perceived that the mother of the future redeemer of Israel (i.e., Moses) was with child, and that this redeemer was destined to suffer punishment through water. Not knowing whether the redeemer was to be an Israelite or an Egyptian, and being desirous to prevent the redemption of Israel, Pharaoh ordered that all children born henceforth, should be drowned.

To us, this Midrashic story seems to have exercised an obvious influence on the form of Mt.'s narrative, the underlying motive of which is to show that the prophecy of Deut. xviii. 15 ("The Lord thy God will raise up unto thee a prophet from the midst of thee, of thy brethren, like unto me," etc.) was fulfilled in the birth of Jesus, in whom the narrator saw a second and greater

Moses. Prof. Schechter, indeed, following Winsche, has suggested that the episode of the star is a "homiletical illustration of Numb. xxiv. 17 (There shall come forth a star out of Jacob), which the Targumim refer to the star of the Messiah." But there the star is identified with the Messiah; and, moreover, in Mt.'s narrative there is no direct citation of the Numbers passage, as we should expect if that had been an influential factor in the representation. Another influential idea that may be detected at work in the narrative is the desire to suggest the homage of the Gentile world as well as the essential divergence between the spiritual kingship of the Messiah, and the earthly kingship of secular rulers (such as Herod), who are instinctively hostile to the new force that has entered upon the stage of humanity.

What are the facts and ideas that underlie the narrative as a whole?

(i) That Jesus was born at Bethlehem a fact which is independently attested by St. Luke (cf. also John vii. 41, 42).

(ii) It is not improbable that the episode of the Flight into Egypt may have a basis in fact in some incident of Jesus early life for the following reasons:

(a) it is in accordance with Mt.'s method to frame his narrative on a basis of what he regarded as fact;

(b) because the story is confirmed indirectly by the obviously independent tradition, which is preserved (with very early attestation) in the Talmud, that Jesus brought magical powers from Egypt with which he later worked many miracles. This may very possibly have owed its origin to a distorted version of an oral tradition which may go back to the early Jewish-Christian Community of Palestine and

(iii) the last section of the Chapter (vv. 19-23) implies that the Evangelist belonged to a Christian Community whose members bore the common designation of Nazarene (the characteristically Oriental name for "Christian"). This part of the narrative also attests the fact (which appears in the Lukan account) that Jesus, whilst born at Bethlehem, was brought up at Nazareth. It is worth noting also that the significance of the allusion to the dictum of the prophets, "He shall be called a Nazarene," can only be elucidated by reference to the Hebrew Messianic terms: neser ("shoot"), semah ("sprout"), and nazir ("Nazirite"). In the LXX equivalents, the indispensable assonance is lost.

Additional Note (1) – The Star of the Magi and the Star of the Messiah

In its main outlines the story of the Visit of the Magi to Jerusalem and Bethlehem is probably based upon what the compiler of the First Gospel believed to be facts. It rests upon a historical basis. The wide spread expectation of the coming of a World-Redeemer, about the time of the beginning of the Christian era, and the interest of Eastern astrologers in his advent in the West are well attested, and may well have led to some such visit as is described in Mt. It must be remembered, however, that Mt.'s narrative is governed by an apologetic purpose. It was written for the special purpose of meeting the needs and objections of Jewish readers. As has already been pointed out above, one influential motive at work in Mt. seems to be a desire on the part of the Evangelist to suggest a likeness between the divinely guided career of Moses, the instrument of Israel's redemption from Egypt, and the Messianic Redeemer who saves His people from their sins.

But perhaps the leading motive in Mt.'s narrative, in this section of it, is to suggest the homage of the Gentile world, and the selection of the gifts (gold, frankincense, and myrrh) may have been influenced by passages from Old Testament Messianic prophecy which predict the allegiance of the nations.

It is noticeable, however, that Mt. here does not cite any proof-passages from the Old Testament (in vv. 5, 6, the quotation from Micah is placed in the mouth of the Sanhedrin). If the compiler had in mind the passage in Numb. xxiv. 17 ("There shall come forth a star out of Jacob," etc.), as has been sometimes supposed, his failure to cite it would, indeed, be surprising. But it is to be observed that in Numbers the star is identified with the Messiah, and would hardly be applicable in this story.

It may be, as Zahn suggests, that Mt. regards the episode of the Visit of the Magi to render homage to the New-Born King not so much in the light of a fulfillment of ancient prophecy as a new prophecy, "which indicates that the Messiah Jesus, who has been born to save His own people from their sins, will be sought out and honored by heathen; while the leading representatives of the religious thought and worship of Israel ask no questions concerning Him, and leave it to the tyrant, who enslaves them, to concern himself about the true King of the Jews, and then only with the object of compassing His destruction." On this view, the star and the astrologers the Magi become significant as proof that God uses even such imperfect means as astrology for bringing the heathen to the knowledge of the truth.

The "star" of the narrative doubtless refers to some particular star, or to some unique astral phenomenon which the Magi were led to connect with the birth of the World-Redeemer in the West. The detail about the star "which they saw at its rising" going "before them, until it came and stood still above (the place) where the child was" is, doubtless, not intended to be understood literally. It is merely a poetical description of the illusion which makes it appear that a luminous heavenly body keeps pace, and maintains its relative position, with the movement of the observer.

Various attempts have been made to identify the "Star" of this narrative with some exceptional heavenly phenomenon, and to fix its occurrence by means of astronomical calculation. The most famous of these is that of Kepler (1605), who thought of a close conjunction of the planets Jupiter and Saturn in the constellation Pisces a rare combination which takes place only once in 800 years, and which occurred no fewer than three times in the year 747 A.C. (B.C. 7). But the data are too indefinite to allow of any certain conclusion in the matter. Moreover, the ignorance displayed by Herod and "all Jerusalem" as to the nature of the Star hardly suggests that its appearance would strike any but practiced astrologers.

The association of the birth of great men with such phenomena was a common feature in the ancient world, where astrology was held in high esteem. Thus, e.g., "on the birth-night of Alexander, Magi prophesied from a brilliant constellation that the destroyer of Asia was born." On Jewish ground, we have already seen the same idea at work in connexion with the birth of Moses in the Midrash passage cited above. Edersheim also cites some late Midrashic passages which connect the coming of Messiah with the appearance of a star. But these are of very uncertain value.

The Star of the Messiah. Sometimes the Messiah Himself is metaphorically referred to as a Star, a description which is based, apparently, on Numb, xxiv. 17.

Additional Note (2) – On the epithet Nazarene: He shall be called a Nazarene

Some very difficult questions are involved in the explanation of "Nazarene" in this passage. They have been discussed by the writer in the article Nazarene in Hastings. An important discussion occurs in Dr. Burkitt's Syriac Forms of New Testament Names. The most recent contribution to the subject is Mr. C. Burrage's Nazareth and the Beginnings of Christianity (Oxford, 1914). (The art. Nazareth in E B should not be overlooked in this connexion.)

On either of these views, "Nazorean" has primarily, no local significance. It is true that St. Matthew connects it with the place "Nazareth." The transition may, perhaps, be explained as follows: It is clear from the New Testament data that the term "Nazarene" was an early designation applied to Jesus and His disciples generally. It was, thus, the Jewish (Oriental) equivalent of the essentially Gentile term "Christian". "Nazarene" was not the title given by the Christians of Palestine to themselves, but by others outside the Christian fellowship (they probably used for themselves such terms as "believers," "brethren", "saints," "elect"). In time, "Nazarene" (i.e., Naprevos), which meant "one from the town or district of Nazareth," seems to have acquired a somewhat contemptuous, or, at any rate, hostile nuance (cf. John i. 46). The followers of "the Nazarene" had evidently been made to feel the reproach of the alleged Galilean origin of their Messiah. Moved by these influences, the Jewish-Christians seem to have transformed the title which had now become in the mouths of their opponents an opprobrious one into the honorific one and to have adopted the latter as a substitute for the former. In this way, at any rate, St. Matthew seems to turn the edge of the reproach leveled at the Christian Messiah in the characteristically Jewish Palestinian designation of Jesus as "the Nazarene."

The selection of this particular Messianic term on the view just put forward was dictated by the necessity of finding a counter-term to Naprevos. "Nazorean" is, thus, an honorific title, given by the disciples themselves to Jesus, and expresses the conviction that He was the neser of Is. xi. the "Branch" of Messianic Prophecy. Its application to members of the Christian community naturally followed.

CHAPTER III.THE NARRATIVE OF ST. LUKE

It is hardly necessary to show in detail that the Nativity-Narrative embodied in the first two chapters of the Third Gospel is Jewish-Christian throughout. The matter has been well summed up by Usener in a single sentence. "In the whole tone and character of the narrative" he says, "its leading conceptions, its repeated employment of the Hebrew psalm-form, its familiarity with Jewish and its defective acquaintance with Roman conditions the hand of a Jewish Christian is, as is now generally recognized, unmistakable." It is refreshing, also, to find Usener defending the substantial integrity of the narrative (apart from the supposed interpolation in i. 34-35). Thus, referring to the attempt that has been made to separate the early history of John (ch. i.) and that relating to the birth and early childhood of Jesus (ch. i. and ii.), he says: "To separate the two sections from each other, as has been proposed, is not possible. They are firmly united: Zacharias song of praise points to the Redeemer, and in the prophetic words of the aged Symeon is repeated the same Hebrew psalm form as is seen in the hymns of Elizabeth and her husband."

In the case of one small part of the narrative, however, its integrity in the canonical text is (as has been mentioned) denied, viz., in the crucial 34th and 35th verses of the first chapter. These are supposed, by all the representatives of the advanced critical school, from Harnack downwards, to be an interpolation quite foreign to the context, and out of harmony with the Jewish-Christian character of the narrative as a whole.

In support of this contention, it is urged that in Luke ii the view of the narrative is that Mary was Joseph s wife, and that Joseph was the natural father of Jesus (ch. ii. 32, his father and his mother; v. 41, "his parents;" v. 48, "thy father and I"); the Davidic pedigree of Jesus is traced through Joseph with the harmonistic explanation "as was supposed" (iii. 23); and with this agrees the early reading, apparently preserved in the Siniatic-Syriac, in ii. 5, "with Mary his wife." The narrative in ch i. could be harmonized it is urged, with that in ch. ii. if vv. 34 and 35 which contain the only explicit reference to the Virgin Birth in the Third Gospel could be removed as an interpolation, though there is no external evidence to warrant such a procedure. The excision of these verses as an interpolation is justified on the following grounds.

A closer examination of the suspected verses does not, however, lend any support to the theory of interpolation.

Their phraseology is unmistakably Hebraistic. Thus, the phrase "Holy Spirit shall come upon thee" may be illustrated from the LXX. The verb rendered "come upon" is often used in connexion with "Spirit" and the whole expression has a verbal parallel in the LXX of Is. xxxii. 15: "until there come upon you spirit from on high." The use of "Holy Spirit" (without the article) as denoting the power of God (without imputing to the "Spirit" any personal implication) may be paralleled also from the Psalter of Solomon. To object (as Schmiedel and Soltau do) that, because "spirit" (ruah) in Hebrew is usually feminine, therefore the Holy Ghost (Heb. rtiah ha-kddesh) could not be represented in Hebrew-Christian circles as the father of Jesus is beside the mark. "Holy Spirit" here is an impersonal term, and therefore no question of the sex of the

"Spirit" is involved.

In the words that follow: "Power of the Most High shall overshadow thee" we have, again, an echo of Old Testament language, and, in fact, the whole under lying idea, which is that of a theophany, can only be elucidated from the Old Testament. The verb rendered "overshadow" is that used in the LXX of Exodus ch 35, of the cloud which rested on the Tabernacle when it was filled with the "glory of the Lord." As Prof. Briggs has pointed out: "The annunciation represents the conception of Jesus as due to a theophany." And the method adopted for describing this in the suspected verses is suggested by the language of the Old Testament. "The entrance of God into His tabernacle and temple to dwell there in a theophanic cloud would naturally suggest that the entrance of the divine life into the virgin s womb to dwell there would be in the same form of theophanic cloud."

The verses are of the same character as the rest of the narrative, and must be the work of a Jewish writer; and there is every reason to believe, with Gunkel, that they are translated from a Hebrew original. This consideration will help to elucidate the meaning of the announcement in v. 31 more closely. The Hebrew original of ("Thou shalt conceive") there would be a participle, and the exact rendering would be: "Behold thou art conceiving now," An immediate conception is meant, not one that would naturally follow after Joseph had in due course taken her to wife; and this immediate conception is implied by the words "with haste" in v. 39. Besides, v. 36 ("And behold Elisabeth, thy kinswoman, she also hath conceived a son in her old age") implies that a conception of an extraordinary character has been mentioned in the previous verses in reference to Mary; and the words suggest that a not unnatural doubt and surprise on her part are being set at rest (ch esp. v. 37: "For no word of God shall be impossible"). There would be nothing extra ordinary in Mary s conceiving a son as Joseph's wife.

Again, the Lukan genealogy, far from discrediting, seems to us to offer a positive argument for the authenticity of the suspected verses. Jewish gene alogies usually have some edifying purpose in view, and the list in Luke iii. 23-38, seems to be no exception to the rule. The striking feature about it is that it traces the descent of Jesus right up to "Adam (the Son) of God." Evidently, in linking Adam to Christ, the editor or compiler intends to suggest that Christ is the Second Adam, the re-founder of the human race; and that just as the first Adam was Son of God by a direct creative act, so also was the second (by the power of the Holy Spirit). For genealogical purposes, it was necessary to link Jesus to previous generations through His foster-father Joseph. But the suggestion is that the Second Adam, like the first, owes His human existence to a direct creative act on the part of God. Luke iii 38, thus supports the genuineness of i 35 and the whole genealogy, viewed in the light of its edifying purpose, guarantees the original character of the alleged interpolation.

The fact that the expression "Son of God" in the genealogy involves the occurrence of "Son" in the physical sense of origin exactly as in i. 35, has an important bearing on the objection noted above, viz., that while in v. 32 ("Son of the Most High") "Son" denotes official adoption, in v. 35 it describes actual physical origin. But the two ideas are not mutually exclusive. At the same time, it is difficult to see what can have suggested such an otherwise un-Jewish application of the term "son" in such a context, and amid language so Hebraistic, except the actual occurrence of the fact narrated.

But the theory of interpolation is confronted with a further radical difficulty. It is not enough to remove the suspected verses to make the narrative congruous with a non-miraculous birth. The significant fact still remains that the figure of Joseph is quite subordinated in the Lukan account, while that of Mary is proportionately enhanced in lonely importance. This feature dominates the whole structure of Luke's first two chapters; and in this particular a sharp (and obviously designed) contrast is suggested between the nativity of John the Baptist and that of Jesus. While in the case of the Baptist's birth the annunciation is made to the father (i. 15), in that of Jesus it is made to the mother (i. 38); and while the Baptist's birth is represented as the occasion of such profound joy on the part of Zacharias that the latter's dumbness is overcome, and he bursts into the strains of the Benedictus (i. 68-79), no such role is assigned to Joseph. What reason can be adduced for this deliberate minimizing of the part assigned to Joseph a feature that characterizes the Lukan narrative throughout except it be that the fundamental fact, dominating and forming the climax of the whole, is the miraculous birth of Jesus of a Virgin-mother?

Usener, indeed, partially perceives this difficulty, and therefore supposes a certain amount not only of interpolation, but also of omission to have taken place. "We are," he says, "in a position to infer with certainty from ii. 5 that in the original form of the narrative after i. 38 stood the further statement hardly to be dispensed with (even though judged inadmissible by the redactor who interpolated i. 34 f.), that Mary was then taken to wife by Joseph, and that she conceived by him."

But, to produce anything approaching a consistent result, the present form of the narrative must be subjected to much more drastic treatment. The whole stress and emphasis of the narration must be altered; the prominence assigned to Mary must be got rid of and a hymn of thanksgiving, corresponding to the Benedictus, ought, at least, to be assigned to Joseph. In a word, the symmetry and substance of the Lukan account must be destroyed; it must be torn to shreds and wholly re-written.

Is it conceivable that the "original" form of the narrative can have undergone so radical a transformation as is desiderated by Usener's hypothesis, and yet have produced the present balanced whole? To the writer, such a conclusion seems irreconcilable with the data afforded by a critical study of the account in its entirety. Usener's theory, far from removing difficulties, only serves to raise fresh critical problems. It reduces the Lukan narrative to hopeless confusion, and (in view of its admittedly Jewish-Christian character) involves its genesis in insoluble obscurity.

The Origin of the Lukan Narrative

The Lukan narrative, then, in its integrity, may be regarded as Jewish-Christian through and through. It must have emanated from Jewish-Christian circles, and doubtless reflects the piety and worship of the early Palestinian Christian Church.

What account, then, is to be given of the origin of its present Greek canonical form? One commonly held theory is that the Lukan form is a direct translation from an Aramaic document. But, as has been pointed out by Lagarde, Resch, and Dalman, these early chapters have throughout a coloring distinctly Hebrew, not Aramaic, and not Greek. Dalman, however, thinks that "the assumption of a Hebrew document as the source for Luke i, ii must, at any rate, be held as still unproved; and it might even be maintained" he adds, "that the strongly marked Hebrew style of these chapters is on the whole due, not to the use of any primary source, but to Luke himself. For here, as in the beginning of the Acts, in keeping with the marvelous contents of the narrative, Luke has written with greater consistency than usual in biblical style, intending so to do and further powerfully affected by the liturgic frame of mind of which Deissmann speaks." Dalman, however, goes too far in excluding altogether the use of Hebrew sources in the composition of the first two chapters of the Third Gospel. My own conclusion, arrived at independently, closely approximates to that of Prof. Briggs, whose words may be quoted. Briggs points out that the material of which the Gospel of the Infancy is composed is "in the form of poetry embedded in prose narrative. This poetry is of the same kind as the poetry of" the Old

Testament. It has the same principles of parallelism and measurement of the lines by the beats of the accent, or by the number of separate words. This poetry was translated from Aramaic originals, and was doubtless written when translated by Luke. The Greek translation in some cases destroys the symmetry of the lines of Aramaic poetry, obscures their measurement, and mars their parallelism. It is probable that the prose which encompasses this poetry comes from the authors of the Gospels, the poetry from other and probably several different authors. Therefore, we are not to look for an earlier written Gospel of the infancy of Jesus, but are to think of a number of early Christian poems with reference to that infancy from which the author of our Gospel made a selection. These songs, which have been selected for use in the Gospel of Luke, doubtless represent reflection upon these events by Christian poets, "who put in the mouths of angels, the mothers and the fathers, the poems which they composed. But the inspired author of the Gospel vouches for their propriety and for their essential conformity to truth and fact."

The only point on which I venture to differ from Prof. Briggs is as to the original language of these hymns. This may very well have been not Aramaic but Hebrew. This hypothesis would account for the pronouncedly Hebraistic character of the narrative as a whole. The hymns themselves are obviously modeled on the psalm-poetry of the Old Testament. There is every reason to suppose that a part at least of the sacred poetry of the Old Testament such as the Red Sea Song (Exod. xv.), the special Psalms for the days of the week, and a rudimentary form of the collection of psalms which afterwards bore the technical name of the "Hallel," possibly, also, the "Psalms of Degrees" would be familiar in their Hebrew form to the Aramaic-speaking Jews of Palestine in the time of Christ, from their liturgical use in public worship. We have the analogous practice of the modern Jews to guide us. Though multitudes of modern Jews possess but the barest acquaintance with Hebrew as a language, they are perfectly familiar with, and sing with the utmost zest, their popular hymns such as Yigdal and En Kelohenu in their Hebrew form. 1 There is also the precedent of the so-called Psalter of Solomon. The remarkable resemblances in phraseology and diction between these "Psalms" and the Songs in St. 1 Luke (the Magnificat, the Benedictus, the Angelic Hymn, and the Nunc Dimittis) have been pointed out in detail by Ryle and James in their classical edition of the Psalms of Solomon. These editors give good reasons for supposing that the Psalms in question were "intended for public and even for liturgical use," and argue strongly for a Hebrew original. Exactly the same arguments may be applied to the hymns of the Nativity Narratives. We conclude, therefore, that these hymns were composed in classical Hebrew for; liturgical use, and were so used in the early Jewish- Christian Community of Palestine and this conclusion accords with their primitive Christology, which betrays no knowledge of the Logos-doctrine of the Prologue to the Fourth Gospel, for instance.

The selection of the hymns and their setting in the prose narrative, with its "scenic" features and schematic and dramatic arrangement, betray the hand of the Greek historian, and are doubtless due to St. Luke himself.

The only serious argument known to us that militates against the view here advocated is the objection of Dalman that the expression ("whereby the dayspring from on high hath visited us," Luke i. 78, in the Song of Zacharias) is formed "entirely after the Greek Bible and quite impossible to reproduce in Hebrew." It is clear that the word rendered "Dayspring" could only go back to the Hebrew Semah, the word rendered "shoot" or "branch" and applied to the Messiah (Jer. xxiii, 5; Zech. iii. 8, vi. 12). But, according to Dalman, "the Hebrew Semah (shoot) excludes the allusion to the light which follows in v. 79." Therefore, he concludes: "it is clear that in Luke, ch. i. an original in Greek lies before us." But it may be doubted whether an original Hebrew Semah in such a connexion would be involved in such disabilities. As is well known, Semah ("Branch") was a common designation of the Messiah, and is used practically as a proper name and as Dalman himself points out, it is actually rendered in the Targum by the term "Messiah" (in Is. iv. 3). As such, of course, it could well be made the subject of such a verb ("visited").

But the question remains, is such a personal designation of the Messiah incompatible with the metaphor of light that immediately follows ("where by the Semah from on high hath visited us to give light to them that sit in darkness")? The meaning of the word in Hebrew is not exactly "branch," but "shoot" or "offspring" (lit. what sprouts or springs up). Now it is significant that in Syriac both the verb Semah and the noun semha are constantly used of light and splendor, and associated ideas ("effulgence" in Heb. i. 3, and is directly applied to Christ). The Hebrew word Semah may, thus, very well have been used here by Aramaic-speaking Jews in the Aramaic sense of "shining." Of this interpretation of the Hebrew term there may also be a trace in the LXX of Is. iv. 3, where the expression translated "The branch (semah) of the Lord shall be" (which was understood of the Messiah) is rendered. ("God shall shine"); i.e., the LXX Here (as often elsewhere) has interpreted a Hebrew word by an Aramaic parallel. It should be noted also that in the Hebrew of the Midrash the verb semah actually occurs with the meaning "shine," "grow bright."

This association of the idea of light with the Messianic designation semah was, perhaps, facilitated by the conception of the Messianic light founded upon Is. Ix. 1 while in the New Testament itself we have in Rev. xxii. 16, the remarkable identification of Jesus "the root and offspring of David" with "the bright, the morning star" (i.e., the Star of the Messiah, Numb. xxiv. 17).

It may be concluded, then, that the original of boys ("Dayspring from on high") was semah mimmarom; that this was a well-under stood personal designation of the Messiah; that with it was associated the idea of light (possibly the light of the Messianic Star), while together with this idea that of the "sprout" or offspring was also included in the conceptual content of the expression; and that the phrase semah mimmarom (i.e., "Dayspring from on high") is a poetical equivalent of Messiah from heaven.

Relation of the Lukan and Matthaean Nativity-Narratives

That the Nativity-Narratives in the First and Third Gospels are essentially independent has already been indicated. But the fundamental facts on which they agree, and on which they revolve, may very well have been derived from a common source, viz., the early Jewish-Christian Community of Palestine. The meagre historical content of Matthew's narrative is explained by the apologetic and polemical purpose that dominates it. He selects and uses only such material as is immediately useful for the practical purpose he has in mind and, in view of this, it is surely unsafe to argue from his silence that he was unacquainted with other traditional incidents which were treasured in the Palestinian circle. And, in fact, there is, we believe, one direct point of contact between the two narratives which suggests that Mt. was not unacquainted with the Hebrew hymns and poetical pieces which are so striking a feature of the Lukan account. Mt. is here using and translating from a poetical piece in Hebrew, derived, doubtless, like the hymns in Luke, from the Palestinian Community; and this conclusion is confirmed by the explanation of the name Jesus, which (as already mentioned) can only be elucidated by a play upon words in Hebrew (not Aramaic).

The significant omission in Luke's account to ascribe to Joseph any part either in the reception or utterance of the "songs," is thus, partially at any rate, compensated for in Mt.

CHAPTER IV. THE NARRATIVE OF LUKE (II)

The episodes described in Luke ii, in connexion with the birth of Jesus, raise many questions, which, in view of the extensive literature that exists on the subject, need not be fully discussed here. Some points, however, which call for remark may be referred to briefly in passing.

(1) The Birth at Bethlehem

The circumstances attending the actual birth of Jesus at Bethlehem are set forth as follows (Luke ii. 1-7): Now it came to pass in those days, that a decree went forth from Caesar Augustus that all the world should be enrolled. This was the first enrolment made when Quirinius was Governor of Syria. And all went to enroll themselves, every one to his own city. And Joseph also went up from Galilee out of the city of Nazareth, into Judaea, to the city of David, which is called Bethlehem, because he was of the house and family of David; to enroll himself with Mary, who was betrothed to him, being great with child. And it came to pass, while they were there, the days were fulfilled that she should be delivered. And she brought forth her first-born son; and she wrapped him in swaddling clothes, and laid him in a manger, because there was no room for them in the inn.

As is well known, the accuracy of the historical statements here made by St. Luke has been confidently challenged by radical criticism in the past. Such criticism took a very unfavorable view of St. Luke's trustworthiness as a historian, generally. And, in particular, it alleged that in the passage cited above, the writer of the Third Gospel had fallen into a series of colossal blunders. Quirinius was Governor of Syria in A.D. 6, and an enrolment, which provoked great disturbances, was then made, as Josephus attests (Ant. i. 1, ii. 1). As Jesus was born in the reign of Herod the Great, who died in B.C. ten years before the Governorship of Quirinius St. Luke must have misdated the latter by a considerable number of years. Further, it is urged that, even if held elsewhere, no such enrolment could have taken place in Palestine during the time of

Herod, because Palestine was not yet a Roman province (as it afterwards became in A.D. 8), and, as Josephus shows (Ant. xv. x. 4; xvi. ii. 5; xvn. ii. 1, xi. 2), Herod was free to act independently in matters of taxation. Lastly, such an enrolment would not at any time have necessitated a journey from Nazareth to Bethlehem, nor would it have required the presence of the wife, but only of the husband, at the place of registration. These positions were subjected to strong criticism by Professor Ramsay, in 1898, in his striking book, Was Christ born in Bethlehem and within the years that have since elapsed, his contentions, and those of other scholars (mainly English), who have helped to vindicate St. Luke, have received strong confirmation, on the whole, from archaeological discovery and research. It was clear from the first that St. Luke, who knew of the later enrolment under Quirinius in A.D. 6 (Acts v. 37), postulates an earlier enrolment, in the reign of Herod, which he carefully distinguishes by applying to it the word "first." The fresh evidence that has come to light, though it does not absolutely prove that such an enrolment as St. Luke attests was actually held, yet makes it probable that one may have taken place in B.C. 10-9 or thereabouts. The editors of the Oxyrhyncus Papyri, Grenfell and Hunt, state the matter as follows ----

"Prof. Ramsay is on firm ground when he justifies from the evidence of Egyptian papyri St. Luke's statement that Augustus started, in part at any rate of the Roman world, a series of periodic enrolments in the sense of numberings of the population; and since the Census which is known to have taken place in Syria in A.D. 6-7 coincides with an enrolment year in Egypt, if we trace back the fourteen year cycle one step beyond it is primed facie a very probable hypothesis that the numbering described by St. Luke was consistent with a general census held in B.C. 10-9. Moreover the papyri are quite consistent with St. Luke s statement that this was the first enrolment."

These deductions are accepted as very probable by the German editors of Papyrus Kunde, Mitteis and Wilcken. The objection that Augustus would not interfere with Herod's subjects on such a matter is untenable. As Plummer points out, Augustus did issue orders about the taxation of the Samaritans after the revolt against Varus, and before Palestine became a Roman province. "If he could do that, he could require information as to taxation throughout Palestine and the obsequious Herod would not attempt to resist."

The purpose of the "first" enrolment was, however, probably not fiscal at all. It was simply an enumeration of persons by households, and had no direct connexion with taxation, which was normally fixed in accordance with a system of annual returns dealing with the value of property and stock. It is true that the enrolment returns did serve to determine who were liable to the poll-tax the "tribute" of Matt. xxii. 17 which was demanded of all male subjects between the ages of fourteen and sixty. But it is hardly probable that any such use was made of the returns of the "first" enrolment referred to in the passage we are discussing. "First," here, no doubt means first of a series, which went on regularly at intervals of fourteen years, as has been pointed out above. It is important to remember that this "first" enrolment must have possessed a peculiar character of its own. It was something new, and, in the case of a subject-kingdom ruled over by a native prince, such as Judaea was ml 10-9 B.C., it would, no doubt, be introduced in its simplest and most innocuous form, as a numbering of the population only. The second enrolment which took place fourteen years later, and coincided with the incorporation into the Empire of Judaea as a province, under the direct rule of a Roman Governor (A.D. 6-7), was accompanied by a valuation of property (for purposes of taxation) an innovation that led to grave disturbances, which made it long remembered, and invested it with special importance (cf. Acts v. 37).

Another interesting piece of evidence from the papyri makes it clear that people were required to return to their regular places of domicile for the purposes of enrolment. The papyrus in question is dated A.D. 104, "It is a rescript from the Prefect of Egypt requiring all persons who were residing out of their own names to return to their homes, in view of the approaching census." The British Museum Editors (Dr. Kenyon and Mr. H. I. Bell) proceed to observe: "The analogy between this order and Luke ii. 1-5 is obvious." No doubt, strict analogy requires that Bethlehem should have been the permanent home of Joseph before the Nativity. And, as Grenfell and Hunt suggest, this may possibly have been the case. St. Matthew's narrative, which represents the point of view of Joseph, does certainly seem to imply that Bethlehem was the home of the latter, before the Nativity. Joseph and his family, according to this account, only migrate to Nazareth later (Matt. ii. 22 f.). Combining the two accounts of St. Matthew and St. Luke, which, as has been argued in previous chapters, undoubtedly reflect older tradition current in early Jewish-Christian Palestinian circles, and which supplement each other, we may infer that Nazareth was the original home of Mary, and Bethlehem of Joseph; that at the time when the edict was issued Joseph was absent (perhaps only temporarily) from Bethlehem, in Nazareth, the home of his affianced wife; and that, in consequence of the edict, he found it necessary to return to Bethlehem. It may be suggested that, unless he wished to repudiate Mary in the condition in which she then was, he was obliged to take her under his protection as his wife (i.e., according to Oriental custom, to make the marriage complete); it thus became necessary for Mary to accompany him. For some reason many can be thought of Joseph s home in Bethlehem was not available on their arrival, and the birth took place in the circumstances described in Luke ii. It may be inferred that, though they ultimately returned to Nazareth "their own city" (Luke ii. 39) their stay in Bethlehem was prolonged for some little time, sufficient in fact to allow for the events recorded in Luke ii. 22-38. Possibly Joseph already had in mind to make his home in his wife's native place, Nazareth, before the journey back to Bethlehem. If so, however, the circumstances attending his marriage to Mary would have made a change of plan natural, not to say necessary.

To avoid scandal, it was imperative that husband and wife should, for a time at any rate, find a home elsewhere. Under such circumstances, Joseph may well have determined to return to his native-place, Bethlehem, and resume his home-life there, with Mary as his wife. He may, possibly, have possessed there a small property a house with some land which, after an absence lasting at least some months, may not have been available immediately on their arrival. Hence, resort to the "inn" or Khan, the crowded condition of which will be explained if we can assume that the time of year coincided with the flocking of the pilgrims to Jerusalem to attend one of the great feasts. The crowded condition of the Khan is, perhaps, read into the narrative, as Spitta points out. The usual view that the "Khan" was full of persons who had arrived in Bethlehem for enrolment is a fantastic one. It is not probable that there was any great movement of population throughout Palestine in consequence of the enrolment. The normal procedure would be to enroll in one s own district. We have already suggested above that Joseph may have had some small property in Bethlehem, and this view is regarded by Spitta as by no means improbable. If that were the case, it would be a natural thing for him to enroll himself there, in accordance with the rule which is expressed by the Roman jurist Ulpian (beg. of 3rd cent.).

Spitta, however, denies that there is any question of a "Khan," or "inn," in the narrative at all. By the end, he understands a building where they had found lodging; and St. Luke s statement means, that because there was no other place available in this abode, they laid the child in the manger, i.e., the manger was in was no other suitable spot within it where they could lay the child. There is no question of the manger being outside. All that implies "is a place where burdens are loosed and let down for a rest." The narrator, Spitta thinks, conceived it as a sort of shed, used for the animals who were at the time out at pasture (and so the manger was free). It would be a spot familiar to the shepherds. But why may not the "card" have been a cave, used for this purpose by the shepherds, and containing a manger? In the Test, of Job, Ch. xi it is related of Job's wife that she "departed into the city and entered a certain cattle-fold, and slept near a manger."

Thus, if the reconstruction of events just sketched be accepted, it may be assumed that it was Joseph's intention to make his home once more permanently in Bethlehem. Not improbably this intention was partially carried out. The Holy Family may well have remained in Bethlehem, as the First Gospel suggests, for a considerable time, perhaps at least a year. Then the events occurred which made it expedient to remove the young child outside the pale of Herod's jurisdiction.

That the circle to which Joseph, a descendant of the House of David, belonged looked upon the circumstances accompanying the birth of a son to him as in some degree extraordinary, is very clearly reflected in both Nativity-Narratives. That Messianic expectations should have been excited in such circles by the event is by no means extra ordinary. If these hopes, by some means, became known to Herod, Bethlehem would clearly be no safe place as the permanent home of the young child. According to St. Matthew, Herod's suspicions were first aroused by the inquiries of the Magi, whose visit to Bethlehem may not have taken place for some months after the birth. It thus became necessary to seek a new home for the young child. Ultimately, as we know, this was found in Nazareth, Mary's "city." St. Luke's account certainly, at first sight, seems to imply that the migration from Bethlehem back to Nazareth took place a short time after the birth, viz., "When they had accomplished all things that were according to the law of the Lord" (ii. 39) i.e., the circumcision and presentation in the Temple. In the First Gospel, however, as is well known, a longer interval is desiderated, sufficient, in fact, to bridge the years that elapsed before Herod's death in 4 B.C. During this period, we are told Joseph and his family took refuge in Egypt, and only returned to Galilee and Nazareth on the accession of Archelaus to the Tetrarchy of Judaea (4 B.C.). The motive suggested for the journey to Egypt is adequate, as well as the reason given for delay in returning. It is quite in accordance with Herod's character that he should have taken measures of the kind described in Mt. ii. 16 f., to blight any hopes that may have been formed in connexion with the birth of a child to a Davidic family however obscure in Bethlehem, if he had, by some means or other, come to know of these hopes. But why, it may be asked, did not Joseph return at once with his family to Galilee? The answer is obvious. Galilee was part of Herod s dominions, and remained so till his death. Only at Herod s death was it made into a separate Tetrarchy. Thus, the story given in the First Gospel accords with the facts. Galilee and Nazareth only became a safe refuge after the break up of the Herodian dominions in 4 B.C. If the birth is placed in 9 B.C., the interval will amount to five years. Though St. Luke apparently has no know ledge of a sojourn in Egypt before the migration to Galilee, his language, which is studiously vague, does not preclude the possibility of such an episode in the early life of Jesus.

When the general character of the narratives is taken into consideration their independence, as well as their strict sobriety and restraint the fact that they are mutually complementary is of impressive significance. The misplaced ingenuity often shown by harmonists in the past in attempts to dovetail together incidents in the Gospel narratives, on the basis of purely arbitrary reconstruction, has rightly been reprobated by sober critical scholarship. But, in the problem we are considering, such an attempt is justified. The narratives are admittedly fragmentary in character; they are written from two points of view which reflect the positions of Joseph and Mary. Their mutually complementary character, which is obviously undesigned, thus becomes one more evidence of their essential historicity, and we are justified in treating them as parts of a single whole, especially as the process of adjustment does not involve any questions of minute detail. Thus, the first and most famous harmonist of the Gospels, Tatian, in the Diatessaron, has combined the two Gospel accounts in a way which appears to possess the merit both of simplicity and verisimilitude. He arranges the incidents in the following order ---

1. The Birth at Bethlehem.

2. Removal from the stable to a house.

3. The presentation in the Temple and recognition by Simeon and Anna (forty days after the birth).

4. Return from Jerusalem to Bethlehem.

5. About a year later, the Visit of the Magi to Bethlehem, and the appearance of the Star.

6. The Flight into Egypt, the result of a divine warning.

7. The Massacre of the Innocents at Bethlehem after the flight of the Holy Family.

8. The Holy Family returns to Bethlehem, perhaps with the intention of settling there permanently, but, warned once again, goes back to Nazareth.

About this reconstruction there is nothing arbitrary; it clearly demonstrates that no essential antagonism exists between the two narratives.

To return, after this digression, to Luke ii 1-5, we have still to refer to the difficult questions concerning the Governorship of Quirinius and the chronology. Did Quirinius govern Syria before A.D. 6-7? It is now widely recognized that this was, in fact, the case. Thus, Mommsen accepts the earlier Governorship, though he dates it 3-2 B.C. This date would not, of course, harmonize either with the Census or the reign of Herod. Sir William Ramsay, however, has been able to produce some new and important evidence, discovered by himself, which suggests that Quirinius was governing Syria in the years 10-7 B.C. This evidence is contained in an inscription found on the site of the ancient Antioch, in Asia Minor, which mentions Quirinius by name as duumvir ----

"Quirinius was elected chief magistrate (duumvir) of the Colony Antioch; and he nominated Caristanius as his prefectus to act for him. This sort of honorary magistracy was often offered to the reigning Emperor by colonies; but in such cases the Emperor was elected alone without a colleague. Under the earlier Emperors, and especially under Augustus, the same compliment was sometimes paid to other distinguished Romans, chiefly members of the Imperial family. Exceptional cases occur in which the field of choice was wider. This inscription is the most complete example of the wider choice it mentions two such cases both Quirinius and Servilius were elected in this way." Why was Quirinius, a man of humble origin, selected for so high a dignity? There must have been some special reason. Ramsay explains this as follows ----

"He had neither Imperial connexion nor outstanding reputation to commend him to the Antiochian coloni. But everything is clear when we remember that he conducted the war against the Homonades. Antioch was a fortress intended to restrain the depredations of the mountain tribes; and the Homonades must have been a constant danger to the country which it was Antioch s duty to protect. It was at that time that they elected Quirinius a duumvir."

Ramsay shows that any year about 9 to 7 B.C. would be suitable for the duumvirate of Quirinius, and that Quirinius probably came to Syria in the summer of 11 B.C., "immediately after his consulship," in order to prepare for the campaign against the Homonades, which could not well begin before June of the following year. His command, which was essentially of a military character, lasted, according to Ramsay, from 11 to 8 B.C., "possibly even a year longer" and that of Saturninus from 9 to 6 B.C.

"As Quirinius was much occupied per Ciliciam (Cilicia was at that time attached to the province of Syria), Saturninus was sent to administer the domestic affairs of Syria and Palestine, as Josephus shows."

It is well known that Tertullian (adv. Marc. iv. 19) states that Jesus was born when Saturninus was Governor, i.e., between the years 9 and 6 B.C. Ramsay would harmonize the two apparently conflicting data by the hypothesis that both Quirinius and Saturninus were governing Syria at the same time, but each administering a different department of affairs, one military, the other civil. He thinks "the enrolment must have been to some extent under his (Saturninus s) charge (and so Tertullian is justified); but Quirinius was in military command, and household enrolments had to the Romans rather a military connexion (and so St. Luke also is justified)."

Ramsay has not proved these contentions; but he has made out a case for them. Some, however, may prefer to suppose that a change of Governors took place during the Census-year, in which case it would be equally true to say that the Census took place "while Quirinius was Governor," or "while Saturninus was Governor." Or, it may be suggested that St. Luke, while right on the whole, has yet made a mistake as to the Governor's name. What may safely be dismissed is the view, which has been made quite untenable by the most recent discussion and research, that St. Luke's statements as to the early enrolment, and its connexion with Our Lord's birth at Bethlehem in Herod's reign, are entirely baseless; are, indeed, pure fiction, the product of a series of colossal historical blunders.

(2) The Annunciation to the Shepherds

(Luke ii. 8-20)

The angelic communication of the Messiah's birth to the shepherds is made, as was the annunciation to the Virgin-Mother, to the accompaniment of a theophany. Such theophanies, as Dr. Briggs points out, "are frequently mentioned in the story of the Exodus."

The first thing to notice about this piece is, that, like other pieces embodied in the Lukan Nativity-Narrative, it is poetical both in structure and character. The Greek, when translated back into Hebrew, forms a series of 7-2 long lines, marked by characteristic rhythm and parallelism. The parallelism is most perfect in the refrain, where heaven and earth, glory and peace, God and men well-pleasing to God, balance each other.

And, secondly, it is thoroughly Jewish-Christian, both in thought and outlook. The spirit that pervades it is that of Old Testament Messianic at its highest. The Messiah who is born, not in David's palace, but in a manger in David's city, is Lord in accordance with the Messianic conception expressed in Ps. ex. 1-2.

He is also Savior (i.e., the Messianic King, Son and Heir of David), who will "save;" His people from their sins, and inaugurate the reign of Peace throughout the world, in accordance with the ancient prophetic view. The Messianic King will be "Prince of Peace."

The poem, with its prose setting, is Jewish-Christian through and through, and is doubtless a product of the primitive tradition to which the other poetical pieces that are so characteristic a feature of the Lukan narrative, belong. The assertion of Soltau that "no Jewish-Christian would really have understood the idea that the birth of the Messiah heralded the dawn of a reign of peace for the whole world and of happiness for all mankind" can only be characterized as an extra ordinary example of critical perversity. We are asked to believe that the true origin of the angelic hymn is to be found in heathen laudatory inscriptions, giving directions as to the celebration of the birthday of Augustus, in which "Augustus is glorified as savior of the whole human race, as one in whom Providence has not only fulfilled, but even surpassed the wish of all men." "For peace prevails upon earth, harmony and order reign. Men are filled with the best hopes for the future, with joyful courage for the present." Soltau proceeds ---

"We see here that the rejoicings at the birth of Augustus found expression in the same way as, we are told in Luke ii. 10 f., the joy of Jesus birth did. This and similar descriptions of the happiness of the world after the appearance of Augustus cannot, therefore, have been unknown to the Evangelist when he wrote the words found in Luke ii. 8-20. The writer transferred them to the times when his Savior was born."

If anything is certain, as our previous discussion has shown, it is that this and other similar sections of the Lukan narrative are Jewish-Christian through out. It is sufficient to say that Soltau s position, as he himself admits, "excludes the idea that the form (assumed by the pieces in question) was due to Jewish-Christians." He is sure they are "not of Palestinian origin!"

Much greater insight and feeling for the genius of the narrative are displayed by Gressmann in his interesting essay on the section of St. Luke we are discussing. Though he strongly maintains the view that the story of the Birth at Bethlehem is pure legend, and cannot be regarded as falling within the domain of sober history, he is equally emphatic in affirming its Jewish-Christian character. The legend is old, and not to be regarded as the creation of the Evangelist, but as derived from popular tradition. Its form is thoroughly Jewish. Even such expressions as "bring good tidings" and "Savior", which must be regarded as termini technici of the Hellenistic thought-world, have points of contact in the Old Testament, and may quite easily have become naturalized in genuinely Jewish circles in the time of Christ. The only un-Jewish expression that Gressmann detects is "Messiah-Lord" for which a Jew would have written "the Lord's Messiah". Possibly the expression is due to mistranslation.

Gressmann endeavors to avoid the difficulties that beset the hypothesis of late legendary growth by assuming that the legendary development in relation to the early life of Jesus took place quite early, and was already complete before the literary activity of the Evangelists began. It grew up as an oral tradition in the circles of the people. It is the reflex on the popular mind of the immense impression made by the personality of Jesus. After subjecting this section of the Third Gospel (Luke ii. 1-20) to a minute and searching analysis, Gressmann concludes that, behind the present form of the text, an older form of the alleged legend can be detected. In the process of criticizing the narrative as it stands, he makes the most of the historical difficulties about the Census and the Governorship of Quirinius which we have already discussed. He also points out that what seem to be inconsistencies in the narrative, are, he thinks, incompatible with its historicity. These need not detain us now. What is most important in the monograph is the constructive part, where the author attempts to reconstruct the original form of the "legend," and discusses its origin and history. A legend must possess a motif. The most hopeful way of discovering this is by analysis and the use of the comparative method. In its original form, the Lukan birth legend is an example of a "foundling-story," of which there are several applied to the birth of great heroes (Romulus, Cyrus, etc.). The hero is envisaged as a mystery-child, springing from the unknown, having no visible connexion with earthly parents. In the original form of the birth-legend of Luke ii 8 fl, Joseph and Mary were absent. The shepherds simply discover the foundling in the manger. But what was the significance of the manger? It is presupposed that the spot where the child was found must have been a well-known one, a locality with associations that would mark it out as the scene of a wonderful event. Now, it is a well-attested fact that early in the second century a cave in the neighborhood of Bethlehem, in the open country, and not in the town itself, was pointed out as the scene of the Nativity. Justin Martyr says ----

The child was born at Bethlehem, and Joseph, because he could find no place in the town where to lodge, went into a certain cave near the town. And while they were there, Mary brought forth Christ, and laid him in a manger, where he was found by the wise men that came from Arabia.

From the fact that no mention of a cave is made in the Lukan account, while an early local tradition persistently identified the scene of the Nativity with a cave in the neighborhood of Bethlehem, Gressmann concludes that the cave in question was a marked spot, with special associations, before the "Legend" of Christ's Nativity was attached to it. The later association of the birth-legend was made easy by the identification of the manger and cave. Cave-stables are fairly common in Palestine, Conder says: "Such stables I have planned and measured at Tekoa, Aziz, and other places south of Bethlehem, and the mangers existing in them leave no doubt as to their use and character." Such a cave-manger, in the open country, away from the town, suits the original "legend." Gressmann proceeds ----

"It is true there were also mangers in the Khans but that the cave must be preferred as the scene of (the legend embedded in) the Christmas Gospel admits of no doubt. The inn is situated in the town while the cave is outside the former must have been far removed from the scene of the (angelic) annunciation, while the latter can be conceived of as in the immediate neighborhood. Above all, however, the logic of the legend demands that the child should have been found not in the midst of (a busy throng of) men, but in solitude in some mysterious spot."

'These considerations confirm the conclusion that the birth-legend was already in existence before it was transferred, in a modified form, to Jesus; the original legend was associated with the cave of Bethlehem, in the manger of which, as everyone was aware, the foundling had lain."

Such legends were especially associated with kings, or men who had raised themselves, by their own successful efforts, to the position of kings; from foundling to world-king.

"It may therefore be conjectured that the story which attached itself to the childhood of Jesus was originally the birth-legend of a royal child (Konigskindes). This is confirmed by a second reason. If in the pre-Christian period a legend was current in Bethlehem, which dealt with the birth of a child, it would inevitably attach itself to the (person of the) Messiah, who as the future King of the Jews must inevitably be born in the City of David. When Jesus became Christ and his birth was transferred from Nazareth to Bethlehem, the Jewish-Christians of Bethlehem (or Judaea) honored him by transferring to him the birth-legend of the Messiah which was already current among them."

Gressmann is of opinion that this type of legend was imported from outside into Jewish circles. But it had already been assimilated, and had assumed a Jewish form in the pre-Christian period.

It must be conceded that Gressmann has erected his critical edifice with great care, and has shown much skill and not a little insight in strengthening it against such assaults as have proved fatal to previous structures of the same kind. Will the new edifice sustain the test of a searching criticism? Gressmann sees clearly enough that the narrative in its present form is Jewish-Christian in character. He guards himself against falling into the absurdities of a Soltau. But, in order to be able to deal with the episode as a transformed legend, he is obliged to cut off the introductory historical matter (Luke ii. 1-8) as something essentially foreign to what follows. The statements about Quirinius and the Census, and the journey of Joseph and Mary to Bethlehem have nothing legendary about them. They are either pure fact or fiction. Gressmann is obliged to treat them as definitely unhistorical, and as due either to the inventive genius or to the blundering of St. Luke. Either of these explanations is involved in considerable difficulties. It is incredible that St. Luke can have deliberately invented such a series of definite and categorical statements, and we have already seen that some of the main supports, on which the case for convicting St. Luke of gross blundering depends, have been swept away by recent investigation and research. It has become increasingly difficult to maintain the view that the historical statements in Luke ii. 1 ff., are without foundation in fact.

Another difficulty confronts Gressmann's hypothesis. The central part of the section which he regards as embodying the transformed "legend" contains a good deal of poetical matter, which, as we have seen, is essentially Hebrew in character. In fact, these pieces (Luke ii. 10-12 and 14) may confidently be regarded as translations of Hebrew poems. They are of exactly the same character as the poetical pieces which are so striking a feature in Luke i. The presumption, therefore, is that they belong to the same body of Jewish-Christian tradition. If the pieces in Luke ii 9 ff., are legendary, so are those in Luke i. The whole series must be regarded as the outcome of pious imagination. We have already seen in a former chapter what insuperable difficulties are involved in this hypothesis. How can such a "legend" as the story of the Virgin Birth have grown up in so strictly Jewish a circle? Moreover, the narrative as a whole the entire Jewish-Christian tradition embodied in these chapters is invested with an air of sobriety and restraint is characterized by a delicacy and refinement that are hard to reconcile with the legendary atmosphere. There is undoubtedly a large element of poetry in them; and we must allow for the presence of the idealizing tendency native to a poetical presentment. But the poems, as has been already pointed out, are built up on a solid basis of fact, or what the writers had the best reasons for believing to be fact. Apart from such a basis, their growth and acceptance in such a primitive Jewish-Christian circle cannot be explained.

The whole legendary hypothesis is involved in great difficulties on the question of time. Legends require time for growth and development. Gressmann's particular form of hypothesis is involved in this difficulty. He says ---

"When Jesus became Christ (i.e., presumably, some time after the Resurrection) and his birth was transferred from Nazareth to Bethlehem, the Jewish-Christians of Bethlehem (or Judaea) honored him by transferring to him the birth legend of the Messiah which was already current among them."

The assumptions underlying this statement are worth a close examination. It is assumed that at a comparatively early period, say between the years A.D. 30 and 40, the story grew up that the Christian Messiah whose real birthplace was Nazareth had been born at Bethlehem. Who were the Jewish Christians of Bethlehem? We do not hear of them in the Gospels or the Acts. Yet they must have been an exceedingly influential body in the early Palestinian Church if they were able to win acceptance for such a story, especially at a time when members of the family of Jesus were still alive. Why do we never hear of this story in the Jewish-Christian chapters of the Acts? Ex hypothesi these Jewish-Christians wished to "honor" Jesus by transferring to Him the birth-legend of the Messiah which was already current among them. There was, therefore, no motive for keeping the story secret. If it grew up in the way supposed, it could not possibly have been kept secret, but must have owed its success and ultimate incorporation into the canonical Gospel-Narrative to its wide acceptance at an early date. In view of such a development, the silence of the other New Testament Books is inexplicable. On the other hand, this silence is explained if we suppose that the narrative is founded on facts, which were not published at first, but treasured for a considerable time within a limited circle closely connected with the family of Jesus. Gressmann assumes, also, that a legend concerning the birth of the Messiah was current at Bethlehem in the pre-Christian period. It is an essential feature of this "legend" that the mysterious child should have been depicted as a foundling, who was discovered in a well-known cave in the neighborhood of Bethlehem. What is the connexion of this legend with that of the

Virgin Birth? The two are quite distinct things. If Gressmann s hypothesis is correct, we must assume that two totally distinct legends had grown up respecting the birth of the Messiah in pre-Christian Jewish circles. According to one story, he is pictured as appearing on the scene as a foundling, whose parents are unknown; according to the other, as born of a Virgin. And both stories found their way, in a modified form, into Jewish-Christian circles later.

In the present form of the Gospel-Narrative the foundling-story has been assimilated to that of the Virgin Birth. How was that accomplished? Are we to suppose that the two stones originally existed side-by-side in Bethlehem? Or did the story of the Virgin Birth grow up in Jewish circles elsewhere? It is difficult to believe that such was the case, because both the obviously independent accounts of the Virgin Birth, contained in the First and Third Gospels, converge upon Bethlehem. In this case, on Gressmann's hypothesis, there must have been two stories current in pre-Christian Jewish circles both closely connected with Bethlehem and the birth of the Messiah there, which were entirely divergent in detail and governed by different motifs. If such stories ever had been current, they must have left some trace in Jewish literature. As has been pointed out in a previous chapter, there is not the slightest indication in early Rabbinical literature of the existence of a popular belief that the Messiah would be born of a Virgin. Let us see what Jewish evidence, if any, can be adduced in favor of the foundling-story in connection with the Messiah's birth.

Menahem (i.e., "Comforter") is simply a symbolical name of the Messiah. The representation of him as a son of Hezekiah is an echo of an older exegesis of Isaiah's Messianic prophecies, which identified the promised Child Immanuel with Hezekiah himself. In the extract from the Midrash given above, the ideas present are: (1) Messiah is already born (He is the son of Hezekiah); (2) He disappears mysteriously soon after the birth, the implication being that He will be revealed suddenly later. Exactly the same ideas are attested as present in the popular conception of the Messiah in the Fourth Gospel; cf. John vii. 42 (Hath not the Scriptures said that the Christ cometh of the seed of David, and from Bethlehem, the village where David was?) and ch. vii. 27 (When the Christ cometh no man knoweth whence he is). These two apparently irreconcilable statements mean that the Messiah was to be born at Bethlehem and then mysteriously to disappear for a time, only to reappear suddenly later. Thus, these ideas were firmly entrenched in the popular mind already in the time of Christ. Justin Martyr (Trypho viii.), cites Trypho as giving expression to the same conception.

But Christ, if he is come, and is anywhere, is unknown, nor does he know himself, nor can he be endued with any power, till Elias shall come and anoint him, and make him manifest to all men.

In the Babylonian Talmud 1 Rabbi Joshua ben Levi is quoted as saying that the Messiah is already born and is living in concealment at the gates of Rome; and in the Jerusalem Targum to Micah iv. 8, the Messiah is represented as being on the earth, but because of the sins of the people he is still in concealment.

From a survey of this evidence, it will be seen how very improbable it is that any story which represented the Messianic Child as a foundling or a deserted waif could have grown up in Jewish circles in the centuries immediately before Christ. The tradition that the Messiah was to be born of the seed of David in Bethlehem was too strong to allow of any such development. How, then, is the story of the cave near Bethlehem being the scene of the Nativity to be accounted for? The fact that caves were often used as mangers in the country district around Bethlehem might facilitate the identification, and, perhaps, even give it some claims to be considered authentic. No special interest in the site of the manger is manifested in the Gospel accounts. The fixing of the site in so particular a manner by Justin and the Protevangelium Jacobi implies a later point of view when the passion for denning such had to be gratified. By the time when interest had grown up, the actual event had receded into a distant past. No doubt the Karakva ("inn"), if it were a building of any sort, had long disappeared, and other local changes had taken place. Probably the tradition did not emerge till after the break up of the country s life brought about by the Roman war (A.D. 66-70). That a strong local tradition then arose which fixed the scene of the Nativity in a cave is significant in view of the widespread cave-cultus that developed in the early Christian centuries in Palestine. As Stanley remarks, "it is hardly too much to say that, as far as sacred conditions are concerned" the religion of Palestine became "a religion of caves."

"First in antiquity is the grotto of Bethlehem, already in the second century regarded by popular belief as the scene of the Nativity. Next comes the grotto on Mount Olivet, selected as the scene of our Lord's last conversations before the Ascension. These two caves, as Eusebius emphatically asserts, were the first seats of the worship established by the Empress Helena (Circa A.D. 326-328), to which was shortly after added a third, the sacred cave of the Sepulchre. To these were rapidly added the cave of the Invention of the Cross, the cave of the Annunciation at Nazareth, the cave of the Agony at Gethsemane, the cave of the Baptist in the wilderness of St. John, the cave of the shepherds of Bethlehem."

The fact that the Emperor Hadrian thought it worth while to devastate Bethlehem and plant upon it a grove sacred to Adonis (Jerome, Ep. Ad Paul, lviii. 3) shows that before A.D. 132 Bethlehem was the scene of Christian pilgrimage and worship. Thus, the conditions were present comparatively early which would make it necessary to gratify the demand for a definite site and in response to this, one of the cave-stables which were common in the district may have been fixed upon; or a cult motive, such as often operated in later times may have been at work, and a cave-site selected which possessed earlier religious associations that were suppressed and displaced by the new cultus.

It is noteworthy that Justin Martyr (c. A.D. 150) connects the cave with a passage in the O.T. (Is. xxxiii. 16, lxx.): He shall dwell in a lofty cavern of a strong rock. Plummer (St. Luke, p. 54), suggests "that the cave may be a supposed prophecy turned into history;" but it seems more likely that the citation from Scripture was intended to justify an antecedent belief. Some scholars think the tradition of a cave as the scene of the Nativity is authentic. Because there was no room for the Holy Family in the Khan, they retired "to a stall or cave where there was room for the mother and a crib for the babe." This opinion is supported by the high authority of Professor G. A. Smith (E B, col. 561), who, however, does not believe that the Grotto of the Nativity, which forms the most sacred feature of the present Church of the Nativity at Bethlehem, marks the actual site: "It is only probable," he says, "that Jesus was born in a cave, and there is nothing to prove that this was the cave, for the site lay desolate for three centuries." It is curious that Bethlehem is not mentioned by Josephus after Solomon's time, or in the Books of Maccabees. It apparently was only an insignificant village in the first century A.D. As we have seen, Christian influence had become strong there, possibly as early as the last quarter of the first century A.D., and (as at Nazareth), has remained predominant ever since. When it became a place of Christian pilgrimage, it naturally grew in importance; and at the present time it has a population of about 8,000 (mainly Christian).

Looking at the narrative contained in Luke ii. 8-20 as a whole, we may claim that it embodies a tradition which is part of the entire mass of the Jewish-Christian tradition of St. Luke's first two chapters, and comes to us with the same credentials as the other parts. We are justified, therefore, in regarding it as based upon actual fact. It is conceded that the narrative has been handed down in a poetized form. But this is simply the natural way of expressing some great and impressive experience. It is not difficult to suppose that such an experience actually took place at a time of great popular excitement, when the air was charged with intense Messianic expectations, and at Bethlehem; as Mr. Sweet, following Dr. Gore, observes ---

"We may believe, without surrender of the vital point at issue that the dreams and annunciations, and other machinery of revelation form the poetic accessories and literary draping of experiences so transcendent that the subjects of them could not relate them intelligibly to others, except under the forms hallowed by usage and familiar to those acquainted with the old covenant."

CHAPTER V.THE NARRATIVE OF ST. LUKE (III)

It remains to discuss the other episodes connected with Our Lord's infancy and boyhood, as these are narrated in Luke ii. They are embraced in two sections: (1) the account of the Circumcision and the Presentation in the Temple (Luke ii. 21-40); and (2) an episode in the boyhood of Jesus (Luke ii. 41-52).

(1) The Circumcision and Presentation in the Temple (Luke ii. 21-40)

We need not linger over the reference to the circumcision, which was carried out, in accordance with the Law, on the eighth day after birth, beyond noting the interesting fact that the naming of the child is closely associated with it. This, with the corresponding passage about the naming of John the Baptist (Luke i. 59) is the chief Biblical evidence that naming was connected with circumcision. The verses (22 fl.) which refer to the presentation in the Temple offer some difficult problems of interpretation. The important verses are 22-24, which run as follows: And when the day of their (v. L her) purification according to the Law of Moses were fulfilled (i.e., 40 days after birth ; cf. Lev. xii. 2-6) they brought him up to Jerusalem to Present him to the Lord; 23 as it is written in the Law of the Lord every male that open the womb shall be called holy to the Lord (cf. Ex. xiii. 32; Numb, xviii. 15-16 first-born to be devoted to Jahveh, and redeemed one month after birth for a specified payment) and to offer a sacrifice according to that which is said in the Law of the Lord, a pair of turtledoves or two young pigeons (i.e., the sacrifice prescribed in Lev. xii. 8, for the purification of the mother 40 days after the birth of the child).

These verses, it will be observed, deal with two distinct things: (1) the purification of the mother, which could not take place till 40 days had elapsed from the child's birth (vv. 22a and 24); and (2), separating these, vv. 22b and 23 refer to the redemption of the first-born son, which normally took place 30 days after birth. Neither of these acts required the presence of any of the parties, at this period, in the Jerusalem Temple; and no evidence exists of a ceremony of the presentation of the child to the Lord. These points can best be made clear by a statement of the normal method of procedure.

According to the Law (Numb, xviii. 16) the first born son was to be redeemed from a month old, for a money payment of five shekels. No particular place is specified where this is to be effected, either in the Law or later Rabbinic enactments. In fact, in later usage, the redemption could, apparently, be effected in the absence of the child. The normal practice was, however, as it is today, to take the child before a priest, in any convenient place, make a declaration as to the child's being the first-born of his mother, and pay the redemption money to the priest. In the present form of the rite, after the declaration by the Father (This my first-born son is the first-born of his mother, and the Holy One, blessed be He, hath given command to redeem him, etc.), the Father places the money before the Cohen, who then asks the following question: Which wouldst thou rather give me, thy first-born son, the first-born of his mother, or redeem him for five selaim, which thou art bound to give according to the Law? The Father replies: "I desire rather to redeem my son, and here thou hast the value of his redemption, which I am bound to give according to the Law."

The Cohen (Priest), having taken the redemption money, returns the child to his Father, who thereupon pronounces the following Blessings ---

Blessed art Thou, Lord our God, King of the Universe, who hast sanctified us by Thy commandments, and given us command concerning the redemption of the son.

Blessed art Thou, Lord our God, King of the Universe, who hast kept us in life, and hast preserved us, and enabled us to reach this season.

The Cohen then takes the redemption-money, and, holding it over the head of the child, says ---

This is instead of that, this in commutation for that, this in remission of that. May this child enter into life, into the Law and the fear of Heaven. May it be God's will that, even as he has been admitted to redemption, so may he enter into the Law, the nuptial canopy, and into good deeds.

The Cohen then places his hand upon the head of the child and blesses him (God make thee as Ephraim and Manasseh, etc.). It should be added that, if the father of the child be a Cohen or a Levite, or the mother the daughter of a Cohen or Levite, there is no obligation for redemption. The rite, in its present developed form, was not fixed till the post-Talmudic age. But the two blessings pronounced by the father are cited in the Talmud, and the whole ceremony goes back in its beginnings to a much earlier period.

The normal time for effecting the redemption of the child is, as has already been stated, 30 days after the birth. This is clearly set forth in the rubric attached to the present rite which runs as follows ---

The first-born child, if a male, must be redeemed on the thirty-first day of his birth. Should the thirty-first day fall on a Sabbath or Holy Day, the ceremony is postponed until the day following.

But, in the prescriptions of the Mishna, embodying the earliest codification of the Jewish Oral Law, provision is definitely made for dealing with cases where, for some reason or other, the redemption money has either not been paid within the prescribed time, or has been paid before the proper time. The important passage, in this connexion, occurs in the Mishna-Tractate (Bekhoroth viii. 6), and runs as follows ----

If a first-born son dies within thirty days, the priest must return the money which has been paid for his redemption, if it has already been received; but if the son dies after thirty days, the father must still pay the money to the Priest, if he has not already received it. If the father die within the thirty days, he (the son) is presumed not to have been redeemed, unless proof can be adduced that he has been redeemed (if the father) die after thirty days, it is presumed that (the son) has been redeemed, until proof (to the contrary) has been adduced.

It is clear from this passage, that exceptions to the normal practice of effecting the redemption on the thirty-first day after birth might, and did, occur. If the parents desired that the ceremony should take place in the Temple and there is no sufficient reason why this should not have been the case during the period when the Temple was still standing it might be desirable and convenient to postpone the ceremony. In the case we are considering, the motive for such a postponement lies on the surface of the narrative the parents desired to combine two ceremonial acts, redemption of the child, and purification of the mother; and the latter could only take place after the lapse of 40 days from the birth. Nor should it be forgotten that the possibility of redemption after the 30 days is supported by the letter of the Law itself (from a month old shalt thou redeem, Numb, xviii. 16).

In the case of the purification of the mother, the Law expressly lays down that when the days of her purifying are fulfilled, for a son or for a daughter, she shall bring her sin offering unto the door of the tent of meeting, unto the Priest; and he shall offer it before the Lord, and make atonement for her (Lev. xii. 6-7). Here, it is clearly contemplated that the mother should be present personally in the Sanctuary. But in the later period, when conditions had altered, a system had grown up which made the presence of the mother in the Temple unnecessary. It would obviously be impossible for every mother, in a land where the Jewish population had grown to considerable dimensions and was widely scattered, to undertake a journey to Jerusalem after the birth of every child, for the purpose of purification. It is enacted in the Oral Law (Mishna Nega im, xiv. 12) that all the necessary duty could be discharged by the husband. This he could effect by payment of a fixed sum into a receptacle, provided for the purpose, in the Temple, which would automatically be expended in providing the necessary offering. All that he had to do was to be careful to see that the payment was made on the proper day. The priests on duty in the Temple were responsible for arranging that all money provided in this way was expended during the day in the appropriate offerings. In the evening of the same day the woman was ceremonially clean, and freed from the limitations imposed upon her by her previous condition.

But these arrangements by no means prevented those who would wish to do so from being personally present in the Temple at the time when the sacrifices were offered. In fact, it appears from the sources that special arrangements were made by the chief of the lay-representatives on duty, at a particular point in the daily Temple Service, for directing the movements of those who were ceremonially unclean, and were present for the purpose of purification. They were ranged at the Eastern Gate of the Temple (Mishna, Tamid v. 6), i.e., "within the wickets on either side the great Nicanor Gate, at the top of the fifteen steps which led up from the Court of the Women to that of Israel." There is no doubt that women, presenting sin-offerings, were sometimes included on such occasions, and, consequently, that the Mother of Jesus could have attended the Temple Service at which her sacrifice was offered. It is well known that private sacrifices as distinguished from the public sacrifices of the whole congregation, occupied a considerable amount of the time and energy of the priests on duty. A further difficulty in the Lukan account is to determine the precise force of "their" in v. 22 ("when the days of their purification were fulfilled"). The Law speaks only of the purification of the mother. It has been suggested that though there is no direct basis for the use of such a plural in the Old Testament Law--   "Yet it may reflect the thought of the first century respecting the meaning of the ceremony. If it refers to the mother and child, the basis for the inclusion of the child with the mother may have been furnished in the implication of circumcision that the child was unclean at birth, or in the necessary contact of a nursing child with its mother; and because of one or both of these, the thought may have arisen that the child shared in the uncleanness of the mother until her purification, and that the ceremony of purification pertained to them both." It is more probable on the whole, that the plural pronoun refers to the mother and child than to the father and mother, though the latter would be the natural construction grammatically. The suggestion of Edersheim that the reference is to the Jews in general is fanciful and unconvincing. But another possibility remains. The character of the diction, and the tone of the whole passage, suggest that the Evangelist is here using a Hebrew or Aramaic document. If so, the awry ("their") may be due to mistranslation based upon a misreading of the possessive suffix in the original. In this case, the implication will be that the translator was unfamiliar with the details of the Jewish Law.

Another point which it is necessary to discuss is the question of the Presentation of the infant Jesus in the Temple. What is meant by to present him to the Lord? The act, as appears from the context, is bound up with that of the redemption. It was an act of consecration, and may be explained as an interpretation of Ex. xiii, thou shalt set apart unto the Lord all that open the womb. It is true Trapao-raffai, is not the LXX translation of the Hebrew word used here, but it may well be an interpretation of it. Such an act of consecration in behalf of a first-born son is thoroughly in accordance with Jewish feeling and the tenor of the Law. The Jewish commentators on Exodus xiii (Rashi, et al.), expressly allow that the setting apart of the first-born to the Lord may apply to the first born of men. It is true we know nothing of a ceremony of presentation either in Jewish law or custom. But the voluntary performance of such an act, especially in the case of one who was the centre of such pious hopes as those that surrounded the infancy of Jesus, would be a perfectly natural expression of that devotion or consecration to the

Lord required by the Law. The somewhat analogous case of Hannah's child, who was devoted to the service of God from before his birth, will at once come to mind (1 Sam. i. 11, etc.). The feeling that the first-born should be regarded as a pre-destined priest is curiously persistent among Jews. Thus, a mediaeval Jewish writer says ----

Our predecessors made the rule to destine every first-born to God, and before its birth the father had to say: "I take the vow that if my wife presents me with a son, he shall be holy unto the Lord, and in His Torah (Law] he shall meditate day and night."

"On the eighth day after the Berith Milah (Circumcision) they put the child on cushions, and a Bible on its head, and the elders of the community, or the principal of the College, imparted their blessings to it. These first-born sons formed, when grown up, the chief contingent of the Yeshiboth (Talmudical Colleges), where they devoted the greatest part of their lives to the study of the Torah." That some such feeling operated in earlier times would seem to be apparent from the language used in the Mishna in reference to the first-born. It expressly distinguishes between the first-born "who is fit for the priesthood" (Heb. Bekhor le-kohen) and the first-born who is only "fit for inheritance" (Heb. Bekhor le-nahala). Only those who came within the first category (i.e., who were not affected with such bodily defects as would disqualify them for the priesthood) were required to be redeemed. The other class might inherit, but were not to be redeemed. If, then, only a child without such blemish could be redeemed, "it would seem almost a matter of necessity that the child should be taken before the priest, and so naturally, in the case of all those living near to Jerusalem, to the Temple. Such a presentation could hardly have followed the payment of the redemption price, but must have preceded or accompanied it."

In estimating the credibility of the passage as a whole, it is important that we should keep in mind the following considerations: (1) we know far too little in detail about the manifold activities that centered in the Temple during the first century of our era to dogmatize as to the non-existence and growth of a pious custom, when such is attested in a narrative that otherwise appears to be credible and ancient. Unless the alleged facts are flagrantly out of harmony with known Jewish usage, it is precarious to dismiss them on purely a priori grounds. It has been shown in the previous discussion that the alleged facts are not out of harmony with known Jewish usage; that, on the contrary, there is much that indirectly supports their claim to acceptance as true. It is important, in this connexion, to remember that the Gospel-Narrative does not state that the presence of the Holy Family in the Temple was required by the Law; it simply alleges the fact that they were present. We know from many other examples referred to in the Rabbinical Literature that various pious customs in excess of the bare requirements of the Law were practiced in certain circles in connection with the Temple. Further, (2) if the writer of this narrative were not basing his statements on facts, and was himself ignorant of Jewish custom, though possessing (as he evidently did possess) knowledge of and access to the Old Testament Scriptures, it is probable that he would have made his references to the Old Testament more exact.

"The very departures from the letter of the Law imply that behind this narrative there lies something besides the bare prescriptions of the Law and the imagination of the writer."

It is incredible that St. Luke can have invented the whole series of incidents. Everything suggests that he derived his narrative from a Hebrew-Christian source. Its Hebrew-Christian character, sobriety of tone, and general simplicity guarantee its essential genuineness. We may, therefore, confidently interpret the sequence of events in the way suggested by the narrative itself. The Virgin, together with Joseph and the young Child, proceeded from Bethlehem to Jerusalem (a two hours walk) on the fortieth day after the birth; the young Child was presented and redeemed, in the presence of a priest, within the Temple-precincts; and Mary made the accustomed offering to complete her purification.

The beautiful figures of Simeon and Anna, the "prophetess," daughter of Phanuel, of the tribe of Asher, form a striking feature in the story of the visit to the Temple. They belong to the pious circle forming a minority in contemporary Israel which included Zacharias the priest, and Elizabeth, as well as Joseph and Mary; and they live in the same atmosphere. We are once again confronted with their Messianic ideals, set forth in poetical form. To the conception of Messianic salvation expressed in the Song of Zacharias, which blesses God for the gift of it a salvation which consists in moral and spiritual redemption the Song of Simeon adds one other great idea; the Messiah whose advent is celebrated is to be not only the spiritual glory of His people, Israel.

In these words, we catch a note of foreboding that the advent of the Messiah will be accompanied by strife and suffering. It will be in the nature of a discriminating judgment, serving to reveal the thoughts of many hearts.

As the writer has said elsewhere, in these poems "we catch a glimpse of a pious circle in Israel who were awaiting the advent of a Messiah who should effect the moral and spiritual redemption of His people; who should reign as a spiritual prince in the hearts of a regenerate people, and so fulfill the old promises made to the House of David; and one who should extend His spiritual dominion to the ends of the earth. These hopes were based and nourished upon Old Testament prophecy, and were cherished within a limited circle who were to be found both among the learned especially among the disciples of Hillel and also among the people. Among the latter were doubtless included some of the more spiritually-minded of the apocalyptists. Doubtless the poems on which this estimate is based are the product, to some extent, of reflection. They exhibit the piety of the primitive Palestinian Christian Church. Their genuinely primitive character and their essential conformity to truth and fact are guaranteed by their whole tone and character, their Christology, and their setting. In them we ought to see, as I venture to think, translations of hymns, originally composed in Hebrew for liturgical use in the early Palestinian Community of Hebrew-Christians."

The figures of Anna and Simeon are doubtless historical, though the story may, to some extent, have been idealized. They could hardly have been invented. Living, as they did, in an atmosphere of pious hope and exaltation, they would easily respond to the Messianic excitement of the little group from Bethlehem which surrounded the young Child.

It is a notable feature that, while the whole narrative obviously reflects an atmosphere of tense expectation, the language is graceful and restrained. There is little that is extravagant about it. Perhaps there is some exaggeration in the description of Anna as a widow even for fourscore and four years, which departed not from the Temple, worshipping with fastings and supplications night and day. Here, the number of the years of widowhood has, perhaps, grown in the early stages of the oral tradition, and the statement that she departed not from the Temple cannot be taken literally. What is meant is that she spent as much time as possible within the Temple-precincts. No woman could possibly have lived within the Temple-area. It is interesting to notice that it is the Temple which is the head quarters of this little group of quietists, not the synagogue. The Temple offered a less restricted arena for a woman's activities, and would naturally attract a "prophetess." This circle to which Joseph of Arimathea probably belonged (Luke xxiii 51), was looking for the Messianic salvation or "Consolation"; of Israel. We are reminded of the mourners of Sion who practice humility, who when they have had to listen to reproach against themselves have kept silent, who have not grasped at material good for themselves. In the same context a saying is quoted which runs: He who is on the watch for (the Messianic] salvation, the Holy One, Blessed be He, will cause him to lie down in the Garden of Eden, as it is said in (Ezek. xxxiv.

15): "I myself will feed my sheep, and I will cause them to lie down." In Simeon's Song, the eager longing for the expected salvation, expressed by the figure of the watchman straining his gaze on the watch-tower, is already satisfied. The watch man can leave his post with a calm untroubled spirit, because at last his eyes have seen the promised salvation.

The atmosphere of the entire section is unmistakably Jewish and quietist. It could not have been invented by the Evangelist. This is fully admitted by so unprejudiced a witness as the distinguished Jewish scholar Dr. K. Kohler, who, while he will not commit himself so far as to guarantee the historic character of Simeon and Anna, yet acknowledges that "these two stories of Luke have the true Jewish coloring."

In vv. 39 and 40, we probably have summary statements which are due to St. Luke himself. He seems not to be any longer translating from the primitive document. Under these circumstances, his silence about any further sojourn of the Holy Family at Bethlehem cannot well be pressed. He may not have known of any such sojourn, and probably did not know of the journey to Egypt. In any case, such details did not interest him. He was concerned, rather, to bring the Holy Family as quickly as possible to the place of their most permanent sojourn, which became "their own city" Nazareth.

(2) An Episode in the Boyhood of Jesus

(Luke ii 41-52)

The story of Jesus first visit to Jerusalem, after the Presentation in the Temple, is told in this section of the Third Gospel. It is interesting as being the only episode recorded in the canonical Gospels of the Life between infancy and manhood. It obviously interested the Evangelist for a special reason the reply to the reproachful question of Mary: Son why hast thou thus dealt with us? Behold thy father and I sought thee sorrowing. The reply that follows is no doubt correctly rendered in the R.V.: How is it that ye sought me? Whist ye not that I must be in my Father's house? The comment that follows: And they understood not the saying which he spake unto them, is significant. Plummer's exegesis is no doubt right ---

"There is a gentle but decisive correction of His Mother's words Thy father and I in the reply, Where should a child be (Set) but in his father's house? And my Father is God. It is notable that the first recorded words of the Messiah are an expression of His Divine Sonship as man; and His question implies that they knew it, or ought to know it."

In the light of the narratives as a whole, the words point unmistakably to the Virgin Birth.

But such a reply took them by surprise. The secret of the wondrous birth had never been divulged to the Child. Perhaps, even, the glamour of it, in the years of commonplace existence that had elapsed, had partially faded for them. Could He possibly be hinting at His own consciousness of a mysterious and divine origin? They could not tell. They understood not the saying. Or the sentence may have a wider significance. They only gradually came to understand all that was involved in the Child's mission and destiny. As Plummer remarks ---

"They learnt only gradually what His Messiahship involved, and this is one stage in the process. From the point of view of her subsequent knowledge, Mary recognized that at this stage she and Joseph had not understood."

Such a touch can only have emanated from the Virgin herself. The following verse (And He went down with them and came to Nazareth; and he was subject unto them and His Mother kept all these sayings (or things in her heart) also betrays the mother's heart. She shows in the words a natural anxiety to remove the impression "that in His reply (v. 49) Jesus resents, or henceforward repudiates" the authority of His "parents" over Him. The verse also bears witness to the impression made upon her own heart by these occurrences. The beauty, restraint, and psychological truth of the whole narrative are a sufficient guarantee of its essential historicity. It is a picture drawn from the life. But critical objections are not wanting. Gressmann, as we have seen, regards it as a beautiful legend. It is pointed out that it is a common tendency to reflect back the greatness of distinguished men on to the years of youth in fictitious episodes, and in such a category, it is alleged, the story of Jesus amazing the Jewish Doctors in the Temple, naturally falls. The whole story is modeled on Old Testament precedents Samuel, who dwelt in the Temple, was a prophet from his thirteenth year (cf. Josephus, Ant. v. x. 4); in fact, the history of Samuel formed the model for the Lukan narrative (cf. 1 Sam. ii. 26, and Luke ii. 52). But all this fails to account for the psychological truth of the story and its simplicity. These could hardly have been invented. The contrasted fictions of the Apocryphal Gospels are alone sufficient to prove this to an unprejudiced mind. The Old Testament narrative may have affected the form, but not the substance, of the story. Such considerations have brought conviction even to so severe a critic of the Gospels as Keim, who says ----

"It does seem to us, after all has been said, that this fine, tender picture, in which neither truth to nature nor the beauty which that implies, is violated in a single line, in which youthful strivings in their truth and error alike, are drawn with such depth of meaning, picturing so completely beforehand the stages of his after life, cannot have been devised by human hands, which left to themselves were always betrayed into coarseness and exaggeration, as shown by the apocryphal Gospels, and even some stories of the youth of Old Testament heroes but only by true history."

ADDITIONAL NOTE (3). Spitta on the Chronological Notices and Hymns in Luke i,-ii

An important article by Spitta on The Chronological Notices and the Hymns in Luke i. and ii which was published in the Zeitschrift fur die neutestamentliche Wissenschaft in 1906, calls for some notice here. Spitta regards Luke i. 34 f., as an addition made to the original source-document by the Editor of the Lukan Gospel, "based on accounts of the birth of Jesus, like that in Matt. i. 18-25," and the view that Mary conceived by the Holy Spirit. He holds that the rest of the source-document knows nothing of a Virgin Birth. This view has already been sufficiently criticized in a previous chapter and need not detain us now. He thinks the Nativity-Narratives embodied in the First and Third Gospels absolutely irreconcilable.

It is, however, his treatment of the chronological problem that is most interesting. Here, he strikes out a bold and original line. He first criticizes the view that the date of the enrolment under Quirinius, mentioned in Luke ii. can be A.D. 6-7. This is irreconcilable with iii according to which Jesus must have been about thirty years old just after His baptism. Since John s preaching activity is dated in the fifteenth year of Tiberius (i.e., A.D. 28-29), Jesus, on this reckoning, can only have been, at the most, 24 years old. On the other hand, Luke iii implies the view that Jesus was born after the death of Herod (4 B.C.).

The mention of Judas the Galilean in connexion with the enrolment in Acts v. 37 suggests that Galilee was the scene of the rising, as it is known from Josephus that this Judas sprang from Gamala in the Gaulanitis, and, therefore, was not a Galilean by birth. Now, Josephus relates (Ant. xvn. x. 5; Bell Jud. n. iv. 1) that a rising, headed by Judas, took place in Galilee soon after Herod's death; and the account given of this, Spitta thinks, agrees well with the reference in Acts v. The account of the same Judas which appears in Ant. xvm. i. 1, and Bell Jud. n. viii. 1, in connexion with the time immediately following the deposition of Archelaus (A.D. 6-7), Spitta regards as an erroneous doublet. Josephus is badly informed of the events that occurred in the interval between the death of Herod (4 B.C.) and the accession of Agrippa (A.D. 41). The enrolment of Quirinius is to be placed in the years 4-3 B.C., when he was Governor of the Province of Syria for the first time. Spitta defends the Lukan account which represents the enrolment as taking place in accordance with Jewish custom, by tribes and families, as probably historical. Such a concession to Jewish prejudices might well have been made at a time when Judaea had not yet formally been incorporated into the Roman Empire. The result reached by Spitta, which will surprise some readers, is that it is probable that Jesus really was born in Bethlehem, and that the journey thither was undertaken in consequence of the enrolment of Quirinius, which took place some short time after Herod's death in 4-3 B.C. Spitta even thinks that knowledge of this fact that He was sprung from the House of David and had been born at Bethlehem played a not unimportant part in the development of Jesus Messianic consciousness.

Spitta, therefore, concludes that both passages are fragmentary quotations from an ancient Hebrew hymn. This may very likely be the case. The Song of the Angels would, naturally, assume the diction of a well-known formula, sanctioned by usage, which fittingly expressed the feeling of exultant praise of God.

Of the other hymns, Spitta regards the Song of Zacharias (Luke i. 68-79) as composite in character. It is made up of two originally distinct poems, which refer to different things; vv. 68-75 are a song of thanksgiving for the advent of the Messiah, while vv. 76-79 refer to the future of his newly born child, John. Only the latter fit the occasion suggested by the prose-setting for the Song. And so with the other hymns. When the contexts are critically examined, none are found to fit. They are purely Jewish songs, which have been worked over and inserted in their present settings by a Christian editor.

There is much in Spitta s study that is valuable and suggestive. But he does not sufficiently allow, it seems to us, for the possibility that Hebrew-Christians would naturally use Jewish forms to express their new faith, and to expound the new truths. That in the process there should be some lack of logical adjustment, some failure in precision of statement, is not surprising. When it is remembered that the forms employed are largely those of poetry, many difficulties vanish. The people who used them as a vehicle of expression borrowed the forms from what lay nearest at hand. But they were striving to express certain convictions and facts. It is the task of sympathetic historical study to get below the surface to these underlying facts and convictions.

ADDITIONAL NOTE (4) On the Chronology

Essentially the same conclusion as Spitta's regarding the date of Jesus birth is reached by W. Weber in an article on The Census of Quirinius according to Josephus, which was published in the Z N T W in 1909. We cannot here follow his investigation in detail.

Briefly, he subjects the relevant material extant in the Antiquities and the Bellum Judaicum to a searching examination, points out certain discrepancies and difficulties, and concludes that two different sources have been used by Josephus, and the presence of doublets has to be allowed for. Judas the son of Ezekias is identical with Judas of Ganlanitis (Judas the Galilean). The final conclusion reached is that the enrolment mentioned by St. Luke in the Gospel and the Acts refers to one and the same event. It was carried out under the direction of Quirinius (Sabinus), who at that time was Governor of the Province of Syria, in the year 4 B.C., between Passover and Pentecost. The disturbances that accompanied it were particularly serious in Northern Palestine (Galilee). The account of Jesus birth given in Luke ii., is essentially correct. Jesus was born about Pentecost in the year 4 B.C., at Bethlehem in Judaea. He proceeds - --

"It is easy to explain why Mary, in spite of or rather because of her condition accompanied her husband to Bethlehem. Nazareth is not far distant from Sepphoris (where the disturbances under Judas reached their height). Joseph belonged to the peace-loving (quietists) in the land; otherwise he would not have enrolled himself in Judaea. For Mary and himself he possessed in Bethlehem a secure resting-place. There he could wait till the storm in Galilee had spent its force. Meanwhile Jesus saw the light of the world, and after he had been presented in the Temple, Joseph with his wife and child could return undisturbed to Nazareth. Public peace had been restored."

In an article published in The Expositor for Nov., 1912 on The Date of Herod's Marriage with Herodias and the Chronology of the Gospels, Prof. Kirsopp Lake discusses the difficulties involved in the commonly accepted chronology, and himself proposes, somewhat tentatively, a new reconstruction. From an examination of Josephus evidence, he concludes that "the year A.D. 35 is the most probable for the marriage of Herod (Antipas) and Herodias, although a few months earlier is not entirely inconceivable."

If, then, we had only the evidence of Josephus to enable us to date the chronology of the Gospel, we should certainly say that it is clear from Mark that the ministry of Jesus was contemporary with the death of John the Baptist, that His death was later than the death of John the Baptist, that the death of John the Baptist was contemporary, or nearly so, with the marriage of Herod and Herodias, and that therefore the death of Jesus could not but be later than the marriage of Herod and Herodias in the year 34-35.

This line of argument suggests that the Passover of 36 is "the latest possible date for the Crucifixion," but how can this be reconciled with Luke iii. 1, according to which John the Baptist began to preach in the fifteenth year of Tiberius (i.e., 28-29), and (inferentially) Jesus Baptism took place a short time afterwards, so that the Crucifixion cannot have been later than 32 or 33?

A study of the evidence seems to raise the question: "whether we ought not to revise our whole conception of the chronology of early Christianity."

Professor Lake suggests that the date given in Luke iii. 1, which is correct, simply states that John the Baptist began to preach in A.D. 28-29.

"This is generally taken to mean that Jesus was baptized in that year. But St. Luke does not say this; what he says is that John the Baptist began to preach in the fifteenth year of Tiberius, and that he continued to do so until Herod, whom he had rebuked for marrying Herodias, put him in prison. He then says that Jesus was baptized by John, and that he, after the temptation, began to preach in Galilee the natural interpretation of these statements is that John the Baptist preached from the fifteenth year of Tiberius to the time when Herod married Herodias (i.e., 34-35), and that the baptism of Jesus was one of his last acts."

We may, then, suppose that the Census of Quirinius referred to by St. Luke in the Birth-Narrative is that of A.D. 6, that Jesus was born in this year, and that His Baptism took place "probably in the year 35," when He was, as St. Luke supposed, in His thirtieth year. One serious difficulty in this reconstruction apart from the fact that it rejects the whole Nativity-Story of St. Matthew, which clearly places the birth of Our Lord within the reign of Herod the Great (i.e., before 4 B.C.) is how to reconcile it with the chronology of St. Paul's life. This is overcome by the hypothesis of a textual error in Gal. ii. If for "fourteen years", we suppose the primitive text to have read "four years", I "the whole chronology of St. Paul can be put ten years later than it usually is so far as the conversion and his history up to the time of his second visit to Jerusalem is concerned."

"That means that the conversion was about A.D. 43, and if so, we shall have no difficulty in accepting 36 as the year of the crucifixion, and thus satisfactorily accepting the obvious and natural meaning both of Josephus and of Mark." This reconstruction ingenious as it is is hardly convincing. It does too much violence to some of the data. Nor can it be said that its interpretation of Josephus evidence about the date of Herod's marriage with Herodias is entirely convincing. What Josephus says is that "Aretas made this [the divorce of Aretas daughter] the first occasion of his enmity between him and Herod, who had also some quarrel with him about the limits of the country of Gemalitis." It looks as though the quarrel, which eventually led to hostilities, gradually grew. The divorce was only the beginning of it. It may not have culminated for some considerable time; and there were other causes. Consequently, Herod's marriage with Herodias may be dated, even on Josephus evidence, at a much earlier time than A.D. 34-35.

The difficulties that beset the problem must be fully admitted, and no completely satisfactory solution has yet been proposed. In particular, the date of the first governorship of Quirinius is uncertain. If Ramsay's arguments respecting this are not accepted, the possibility remains that an error may have arisen in St. Luke's account by the substitution of one proper name for another. And, perhaps, the best solution that has been offered lies along this line. It has been stated admirably by Burton.

"The statement of Tertullian (Adv. Marc., iv. 19) which connects the birth of Jesus with a census held by Sentius Saturninus, Governor of Syria 9-7 B.C., has usually been set aside because of its conflict with the statement of Luke. But the very fact that it is not derived from the New Testament suggests that it perhaps rested on independent evidence; and when we find the other date given by Luke pressing the census back into the very years of the Governorship of Saturninus, it is obvious to inquire whether Luke has not confused the names of Saturninus and Quirinius. Let it be noted that there were two enrolments, one falling in A.D. 6-7, and one about 9-8 B.C., both apparently known to Luke; that there were two Governorships of Quirinius; that the second of these enrolments fell in the second Governorship of Quirinius; and finally that the names Quirinius and Saturninus are at least slightly alike. Is it not possible that, associating the two Governorships of Quirinius and the two enrolments, one of them under Quirinius, he may have fallen into the error of two enrolments, each in a Governorship of Quirinius? If so, the mistake is in the name of Quirinius, not in the fact or date of the enrolment."

On this view, the date of the Birth must be placed in 9-8 B.C. As it is known that there was considerable variety of method in reckoning the years of the Emperors, it is at least possible that St. Luke reckoned the Principate of Tiberius, not from the death of Augustus in A.D. 14, but from the time when Tiberius began, by a decree of the Senate, to exercise in the provinces authority equal to that of the Emperor (i.e., from A.D. 11-12). As St. Luke wrote in the provinces where this authority was exercised, his adoption of such a method of reckoning is not altogether improbable. In fact, as Ramsay has pointed out, the years of Titus, in whose reign, or very soon afterwards, St. Luke wrote, were reckoned from his co-regency with Vespasian, and offer a striking analogy. On this reckoning, the fifteenth year of Tiberius (Luke iii. 1) would begin in A.D. 25, and the Baptism of Jesus may have fallen within this year. If Jesus was born in 9-8 B.C., this would make him at least 33 years old at the time of the baptism, which may possibly harmonize with the vague terms of Luke iii. 23 (And Jesus himself, when he began to teach, was about thirty years of age). How much latitude is covered by the vague term "about"? It may be suggested, also, that St. Luke may not have known the exact, but only the approximate, date of the earlier census, and that this may have affected the accuracy of his reckoning here.

CHAPTER VI. THE BIRTH AND CHILDHOOD OF JESUS IN THE APOCRYPHAL GOSPELS

Though the discussion of the evidence, or alleged "silence," of the other New Testament documents ought, logically, to follow at this point, it may conveniently be postponed till the following chapter, and give place to some slight consideration of the picture given in apocryphal writings of the Birth and Infancy of Jesus. It is, of course, not intended here to investigate, or to attempt to discuss in any adequate way, this literature as a whole. Such a task would require a volume at least. All that will be essayed will be to illustrate from the Apocryphal material the way in which fancy and imagination and dogmatic prepossession work, when uncontrolled by the restraining influence of genuine tradition. The contrast afforded with the canonical narratives will be found illuminating.

While it is true that some representatives of the Apocryphal Gospel Literature may be regarded as possessing an independent value, as preserving some genuine tradition of a first-hand character this is almost certainly true of the Gospel according to the Hebrews yet the majority is of a distinctly lower order. Based, in the main, on the canonical Gospels in their completed canonical form, they bear on their face a decidedly second-hand character. The accretions to the original Gospel-material are largely legendary, and are the product of two main causes ---

(i) The desire, which in some circles assumed the nature of a popular demand, for fuller information about the Life of Christ than that given in the Canonical Gospels.

"This intelligible and not unnatural curiosity was directed chiefly to the facts antecedent to Christ's advent, and to those periods of His life which the older Gospels left in shadow, His parentage, His birth and childhood, and the period after the Resurrection."

Curiously enough, however, no attempt is made in these writings to fill up the gap between the childhood and entrance on the public ministry. The reason for this probably is "the absence of any dogmatic motive" for the formation of such information.

As Findlay remarks ---

"In the main it is certain that the details furnished by the Apocryphal writings regarding matters about which the canonical Gospels are silent, have little or no historical basis. They are in reality Christian Haggadoth, popular stories similar to those in Jewish literature which were framed for purposes of pious entertainment and instruction. The Gospels of the Infancy and Childhood, for example, are full of legendary matter drawn from various sources, or freely invented by the fancy of the writers. Where the details are not entirely imaginative, they have their origin in the transformation of utterances of Christ into deeds, or in the literal interpretation of O.T. prophecies and Jewish expectations about the Messiah, or in the ascription to Jesus of miracles similar to those recorded in the O.T."

"It is necessary, however, to allow for the possibility that here and there in this literature authentic material not derived from the canonical Gospels has been preserved."

"Oral tradition maintained itself for a time after our present Gospels were reduced to writing, and it is not improbable that genuine sayings of Christ and authentic details about His life have been preserved in uncanonical books."

(ii) A much more powerful motive that operated in the production of these writings was the dogmatic interest. They were largely composed in the interests of certain beliefs which were held in certain sections of the Church. Some of these foreshadow tendencies which later crystallized into definite heresies.

Though these Gospels were never admitted to canonical rank, some of them were greatly prized, in certain sections of the Church, for devotional purposes.

"The popularity of the Childhood Gospels was remarkable, especially in the Churches of the East. There the Prot-evangelium was so highly prized as a book of devotion that it was used for reading in public worship, and furnished material for the homilies of preachers. Translations of it circulated in Syriac, Coptic, and Arabic, and, along with other childhood legends, its stories, often graphically embellished and exaggerated, found a place in a comprehensive Gospel of the Infancy and Childhood, the so-called Arabic Gospel "which had a wide circulation, not only in the Churches of the East, but in Mohammedan circles. Passages of the Prot-evangelium stand in the lectionaries of the orthodox Church for use at the festivals in honor of Mary, and of her reputed parents, Joachim and Anna."

We may now cite a few illustrations to show the character of this literature, beginning with the Prot-evangelium, or so-called "Gospel of James." This compilation, in its present form, has been amplified by the addition of a group of incidents dealing with Zacharias, the father of the Baptist. Apart from this addition, it forms a uniform composition and is a well-constructed romance, dominated by certain dogmatic interests. Its main purpose was to safeguard the Divinity of Christ against Jewish-Christian misconceptions, and to provide an answer against those who reproached Christians with the lowly, if not shameful, birth of Jesus. Most scholars assign its composition to the second half of the second century A.D. It is probably the oldest writing which professes to give the names of the parents of the Virgin. The sources of the Book are the canonical Gospels of St. Matthew and St. Luke, parts of the Old Testament (both canonical and apocryphal), and popular traditions both Jewish and Christian.

It begins by narrating how Joachim and Anna prayed that the reproach of childlessness might be removed from them. In answer to their prayers, Mary is born (ch. i.-v.). When Mary is three years old she is taken to the Temple, where she lives till the age of twelve, and she is fed by an angel (ch. vi.-vii. and viii. beg.). Chapter viii then continues ----

And when she became twelve years old, there was held a council of the priests, who said: "Behold Mary is become twelve years old in the Temple of the Lord. What, then, shall we do with her, lest perchance the sanctuary of the Lord be defiled?" And they said to the High Priest: "Thou hast stood at the altar of the Lord; go in, and pray for her." And behold the angel of the Lord stood by, saying unto him: "Zacharias, Zacharias, go forth and summon the widowers of the people, and let them take a rod apiece, and she shall be the wife of him to whom the Lord shall show a sign." And the criers went out through all the region of Judaea round about, and the trumpet of the Lord sounded, and all ran together.

Joseph answers to the summons with the rest of the widowers, and is singled out for the charge of the "Virgin of the Lord" by a dove which comes out of the rod that had been given him, and alights on his hand. He wishes to refuse the charge, because he is an old man and has children: "Let me not become ridiculous to the children of Israel" he says. He yields, however, to solemn admonition, and accepts the charge (ch. ix.).

After this, the priests, wishing to have a veil made for the Temple, summon the undefiled virgins of the family of David, and among them Mary, who is chosen by lot to spin the "true purple and the scarlet"; and with these she returns home, (ch. x.). While drawing water at the well, she receives the Annunciation: "Fear not Mary, for thou hast found favor before the Lord of all, and thou shalt conceive from His Word" (ch. xi.). Then follows the story of the visit to Elizabeth, and at the conclusion it is stated that "she was sixteen years old when these mysteries happened" (ch. xii.). When the sixth month came, Joseph, returning from his work one day, discovers her condition, and reproaches her (ch. xiii.). Then follows an account of Joseph's disturbance of mind about his discovery. His fears and doubts are removed by an "angel of the Lord" in a dream (ch. xiv.). The condition of Mary becomes known to the priests (ch. xv.). The narrative then proceeds (ch. xvi.).

And the priest said (to Joseph): "Restore the virgin which thou received from the Temple of the Lord." And Joseph wept very much. And the priest said: "I will cause you to drink the water of the Lord s reproof, and it shall manifest your sins before your eyes." (cf. Numb. v. 17) And the priest took and gave it to Joseph to drink, and sent him into the hill country and he returned quite sound. And he also gave it to Mary to drink, and sent her into the hill country and she returned quite sound. And all the people wondered that sin was not found in them. And the priest said: "If the Lord God hath not manifested your sins, neither do I judge you;" and he dismissed them. And Joseph took Mary, and went to his house rejoicing, and glorifying the God of Israel.

(Ch. xvii.). And there was a command from Augustus the King, that all who were in Bethlehem of Judaea should be enrolled. And Joseph said: "I will enroll my children, but what shall I do with this damsel? How shall I enroll her? As my wife? I am ashamed to do it. As my daughter? But all the children of Israel know that she is not my daughter. The day of the Lord will itself bring it about as the Lord will it." And he saddled the ass, and set her upon it, and his son led it, and Joseph followed.

The account of the Birth in a cave near Bethlehem follows (ch. xviii.). Here, the narrative suddenly changes from the third to the first person ---

And I, Joseph, was walking, and was not walking; and I looked up into the air, and saw the air violently agitated; and I looked up at the pole of heaven, and saw it stationary, and the fowls of heaven still; and I looked at the earth and saw a vessel lying, and workmen reclining by it, and their hands in the vessel, and those who handled it did not handle it, and those who took did not lift, and those who presented it to their mouth did not present it, but the faces of all were looking up.

(Ch. xix.). And I saw a woman coming down from the hill country, and she said to me: "man, whither art thou going?" And I said: "I am seeking a Hebrew midwife;" And she answered and said to me: "Art thou of Israel?" And I said to her: "Yea" And she said: "And who is it that bringeth forth in the cave?" And I said: "She that is espoused to me;" And she said to me: "Is she not thy wife?" And I said to her: "It is Mary who was brought up in the Temple of the Lord, and she was allotted to me to wife and she is not my wife, but hath conceived by the Holy Spirit." And the midwife said to him: "Is this true?" And Joseph said to her: "Come and see;" And the midwife went with him. And they stood in the place where the cave was, and behold a bright cloud over shadowed the cave. And the midwife said: "My soul is magnified today, because my eyes have seen strange things (mysteries); for Salvation is born to Israel." And suddenly the cloud withdrew from the cave, and there appeared a great light in the cave, so that their eyes could not bear it. And gradually the light withdrew until the babe was seen.

We need not pursue the contents of this writing further. The extracts already quoted and the summaries given will suffice to illustrate the unhistorical character of the matter that has not been derived directly from the canonical Gospels. The entire representation of Mary as living in the Temple is pure fiction and is historically impossible. And the same remark applies to other features. Yet the Prot-evangelium is the oldest and most important of these writings; it was used by the compilers of pseudo-Matthew, the Nativity of Mary, the History of Joseph the Carpenter, and the Arabic Gospel of the Infancy ; and, compared with some of these latter, is sober and restrained in its representation. Thus, take the following from pseudo-Matthew ---

And it came to pass that after the return of Jesus from Egypt, when He was in Galilee and now entered on the fourth year of his age, one Sabbath day He played with the children by the bed of the Jordan. When, therefore, He had sat down, Jesus made himself seven pools with mud, to each of which He made little channels through which, at His command, He brought water from a stream into a pool, and sent it back again. Then one of these children, a son of the devil, with envious mind, shut up the channels which supplied water to the pools, and overthrew what Jesus had made. Then said Jesus unto him: "Woe unto thee, son of death, son of Satan! Dost thou destroy the works which I have wrought?" And straightway he who had done this died. Then, with a quarrelsome voice, the parents of the dead cried against Mary and Joseph, saying to them: "Your son hath cursed our son and he is dead." When Joseph and Mary heard they came at once to Jesus, on account of the complaint of the parents of the boy and the crowd of Jews. But Joseph secretly said to Mary: "I dare not speak to Him; but do thou admonish Him and say, Why hast thou raised against us the enmity of the people, and why do we bear the painful enmity of men?" And when His mother had come to Him she asked Him, saying: "My Lord, what hath he done that he should die?" But He said: "He was worthy of death, because he destroyed the works which I had wrought;" Therefore His mother besought Him, saying: "Do not, my Lord, because they all rise against us." And He, not willing that His mother should be grieved, spurned the body of the dead with His right foot, and said to him: "Arise, son of iniquity; for thou art not worthy to enter into the rest of my Father, because thou hast destroyed the works which I have wrought." Then he who was dead arose and departed. But Jesus, at His own command, brought the water into the pools through the water channels.

As has been already pointed out, the late compilation known as The Arabic Gospel of the Infancy is full of marvels in connexion with incidents of Our Lord's childhood and youth. One extract will suffice to illustrate the character of these stories, which need not be traced in their further development.

Another day the Lord Jesus went out into the street, and seeing some boys who had met to play, He followed them; but the boys hid themselves from Him. Therefore when the Lord Jesus had come to the door of a certain house and saw the women who stood there, He asked them whither the boys had gone. And when they told Him that there was nobody there, the Lord Jesus said again: "What are these whom ye see in the vault?" They answered that they were kids of three years old. And the Lord Jesus cried aloud and said: "Come out here, kids, to your shepherd! Then the boys came out, having the form of kids, and began to skip about Him. When they saw it the women wondered greatly, and, being seized with fear, they suppliantly and in haste adored the Lord Jesus, saying: "our Lord Jesus, Son of Mary, Thou art indeed the good

Shepherd of Israel: have pity on thy handmaids who stand before Thee and never doubted; for, our Lord, Thou hast come to heal and not to destroy." But when the Lord Jesus had answered that the children of Israel were like Ethiopians among the nations, the women said: "Thou, Lord, knowest all things, and nothing is hidden from Thee; but now, we pray Thee, and from Thy kindness, we ask, that Thou wouldst restore these boys Thy servants to their former condition." The Lord Jesus therefore said: "Come boys, let us go and play." And immediately, while the women stood there, the kids were changed into boys (Ch. xl.).

A study of the whole of this literature only serves to enhance the impression of essential truthfulness produced by the sober and restrained narratives of the canonical Gospels. In the latter we feel we are moving within the boundaries of real history, reflected in a genuine popular tradition. The whole matter may fitly be summed up in the words of Findlay ----

"A comparison of the Apocryphal Gospels with those of the Canon makes the pre-eminence of the latter incontestably clear, and shows that as sources of Christ s life, the former, for all practical purposes, may be neglected. The simple beauty and verisimilitude of the picture of Jesus in the four Gospels stand out in strong relief when viewed in the light of the artificial and legendary stories, which characterize most of the Apocryphal Gospels. The proverbial simplicity of truth receives a striking commentary when (for example) the miracles of the Canonical Gospels are compared with those of the Apocryphal writings. The former, for the most part, are instinct with ethical purpose and significance, and are felt to be the natural and unforced expression of the sublime personality of Jesus; the latter are largely theatrical exhibitions without ethical content. In them we find no worthy conception of the laws of providential interference; they are wrought to supply personal wants, or to gratify private feelings, and often are positively immoral (Westcott). In a few of the Gospels which show signs of independence, there may be here and there a trace of primitive and trustworthy tradition; but all such details, which have a reasonable claim to be considered authentic, do not sensibly increase the sum of our knowledge about Christ. The conclusion, based on the comparison of the Apocryphal with the Canonical Gospels, is amply warranted, that in rejecting the former and choosing the latter as authoritative Scriptures the Church showed a feeling for what was original and authentic."

CHAPTER VII.THE EVIDENCE OF THE OTHER NEW TESTAMENT WRITINGS AND THE EARLIEST CHRISTIAN TRADITION (OUTSIDE THE GOSPELS) RESPECTING THE BIRTH OF JESUS

I

What is the relation between the incidents of Jesus birth, as recorded in the First and Third Gospels, and the rest of the New Testament? It is in the argument deduced from the alleged "silence" of these books that the stronghold of the opposition is to be found.

It is asserted that the incidents of the Nativity-Narratives entirely lack confirmation from the evidence of the rest of the New Testament. Not only are these books silent as to the main point the Virgin Birth at Bethlehem but much of their evidence cannot be harmonized with the alleged "facts." The Virgin Birth is ignored by St. Mark, St. John, and St. Paul, both in the construction of the primitive biography of Christ, as well as in the Christology. If it be conceded that the argument from silence may be in danger of being over-pressed, yet it does "seem strange that comprehensive and systematic thinkers, like John and Paul, could construct their doctrines of the transcendence and authority of Christ without distinct reference to so important fact as His supernatural birth." The explanation of this silence is easy. The Virgin Birth formed no part of the Apostolic preaching, and the fact that there is no reference to it in the Acts of the Apostles shows how trust worthy as a historian St. Luke is. In the early chapters of the Acts he professes to give us the substance of the early Apostolic missionary preach ing. The Virgin Birth formed no part of this. Therefore, no reference to it occurs in the Acts, though the same writer devotes the opening chapters of his Gospel to expounding the circumstances of Jesus birth. The same consideration will explain St. Mark's silence. The Second Gospel begins with the opening of Our Lord's public ministry, following His baptism. No account whatever is given of His birth, because this was not dealt with in the Apostolic preaching, and the Second Gospel is a compilation based, no doubt, upon the sermons of St. Peter. This preaching, it must be remembered, was determined by the character, inherent in the apostleship, of bearing personal witness to certain facts. Dr. Headlam well remarks -----

"St. Mark's Gospel is based upon the preaching of the Apostles, the witness that they gave of the things they had seen and known from the time of the baptism of John, and in all probability it was on the particular witness of St. Peter that it mainly rested. Now he could not be a witness as regards the birth, and therefore it would not be part of his normal teaching; and it is significant that St. Luke himself recognized these limits when describing the election of Matthias and the qualifications of an Apostle."

It is certainly significant that no account whatever is given in the Second Gospel of the birth of Jesus. It is clear that the supernatural birth was not emphasized at first. The explicit teaching about it, and the emphasis laid upon it, came later, and then only as part of a larger belief in the Incarnation. But the fact that the secret of Jesus birth was not at first published to the world harmonizes perfectly with the character of the Nativity-Narratives. The story there enshrined, though unmistakably Jewish in its setting and form, would be especially difficult to explain to Jews. And yet it is impossible to attribute its growth to heathen influence. Its Jewish coloring, its primitive Christology, its reserve and restraint, forbid such a hypothesis. Its comparatively late appearance and primitive character can only be reconciled by the explanation that it is based upon facts which were for long treasured within a narrow circle in close contact with Our Lord, and which were only gradually divulged to the Church. And the instinct which dictated this course was a sound one. The supernatural birth is not the foundation of, but in a sense an incident in, faith in the supernatural personality of Jesus. It is because, on other grounds, we believe in the supernatural character of Jesus that we can believe in His supernatural birth. The purpose of the Second Gospel is to show from the public ministry of Jesus, culminating in the death and Resurrection, that Jesus was the Son of God; and in this it faithfully reflected the early Apostolic preaching. It is easy to put a wrong construction upon St. Mark's silence. As has been pertinently remarked ---

"That Mark began his Gospel at the Baptism, is certainly no evidence that the life of Jesus began then. Jesus, of a truth, did not enter the world as a grown-up man. Mark s silence proves absolutely nothing about the youth of Jesus, or else it proves that He had none. If the belief that Jesus was born of Joseph and Mary was an essential element in the primitive Gospel, why did Mark not state it as such? His silence militates as strongly against the critical view as against the historical view. If Jesus was naturally born of Joseph and Mary, and became by a divine election and baptism the Son of God, it was as wonderful and deserving of record as the miraculous birth."

"As a matter of fact, Mark's silence has no bearing upon this question ---"

But if it be conceded that St. Mark's silence has no bearing upon the determination of the question, one way or the other, what is to be said as to the indirect evidence afforded by his Gospel narrative? Is the representation there given congruous with a miraculous birth? It is, of course, admitted that, according to popular belief, Jesus was, during His lifetime and for some time afterwards, regarded as the son, by natural generation, of Joseph and Mary. "And the disciples or some of them shared the popular belief at first (cf. John i. 45: We have found him of whom Moses in the Law and the prophets did write, Jesus of Nazareth, the son of Joseph). It is certainly curious, however, that in St. Mark's Gospel (vi. 2 fl) the people of Nazareth ("his own country") are represented as unwilling to welcome Him as a teacher, and saying: Whence hath this man these things? And what is the wisdom that is given unto this man, and what mean such mighty works wrought by his hands? Is not this the carpenter, the son of Mary, and brother of James, and Moses, and Judas, and Simon? And are not his sisters with us?

The designation of Jesus as "Son of Mary" is decidedly remarkable and unusual. It is probably contemptuous. In the parallel passage in St. Matthew (xiii. 55) it is significantly modified (is not his mother called Mary) and replaced in the parallel passage in St. Luke by this not this the son of Joseph? (Luke iv. 22). In Rabbinic Literature, where the designation "ben" or "bar" is used, it is in reference to the father. The writer cannot recall any instance of a man being called in Rabbinic the "son" of his mother, in this way. There is, of course, the case of Joab and his brethren in the Old Testament, who are constantly spoken of as "sons of Zeruiah" (she being David's sister, according to the Chronicler). This is sufficiently interesting to call for special remark (cf., e.g., the art. Zeruiah in Hastings DB), and may be a survival of the old custom of reckoning kinship through the female line. More significant, perhaps, is the case of Jeroboam, who, though he receives the patronymic "ben Nebat," is said to have been the son of a widow woman (cf. 1 Kings xi. 26) this description being probably a contemptuous one. In the Lucianic recension, the widow woman becomes Troupe. It looks as although the calumny regarding Jesus birth, which was afterwards amplified, in Jewish writings, had already begun to grow up in Nazareth. Does not this point to some peculiar circumstances regarding His birth which had become known in a distorted form to some people at Nazareth? And may not this be explained by Mary's hasty marriage to Joseph, which coincided with the journey from Nazareth to Bethlehem?

A good deal of stress has been laid by radical criticism upon the incident described in Mark iii. 21. [And when his friends (or kinsmen) heard it they went out to lay hold on him for they said, He is beside himself.]

Who these kinsmen were (says Schmiedel) we learn from Mark iii. 31 f . Matt. xii. 46 f. Luke viii. 19 f; they were his mother and his brethren. For the passage is the continuation of Mark iii. 21; they set out from Nazareth and reach Jesus immediately after he has had a controversy with the scribes (Mark iii. 22-30). Even though we choose to regard it as possible that Mary had kept a life-long silence with her son regarding the secret of his birth, and by this assumption to deprive Mark iii. 33 (who is my mother, etc.), of the force assigned to it. Mark iii. 21 (he is beside himself] would still be decisive; had Mary known of the supernatural origin of Jesus, as set forth in Luke i. 35, could anything have induced her to say He is beside himself? The family secret of which apologists speak did not exist.

Such dogmatism sounds very formidable; but it reveals an extremely defective sense of what is psychologically possible. With real insight and fine truthfulness, St. Luke s Nativity-Narrative insists that Mary failed to understand the significance of the startling events connected with Our Lord's birth and development : And they understood not the saying which he spake unto them (Luke ii. 50); Mary kept all these things, pondering them in her heart. The Virgin-Mother had much to learn all through her life regarding her mysterious Son; nor is there any reason to suppose that the exalted moments of her strange experiences regarding Him were consistently maintained. As Sweet well remarks, radical criticism often makes the mistake of "reading the evidence backward."

"Mary labored to the end of Jesus life under certain mental limitations. She occupied the Old Testament view-point exhibited in the Infancy document, and never passed beyond it until after the death of Jesus. There was nothing in the circumstances of Jesus birth to lead her to expect in Him anything but the fulfillment of the theocratic hopes of the circle in which she moved. Her conduct towards Jesus (cf. John ii. 3, 5) cannot be better explained than by the supposition that her expectations in Him were disappointed. She was a thorough Hebrew, and when she saw her son coming into conflict with the authorities of her nation and turning aside to the narrow pathway that led towards inevitable death, she was troubled, perplexed, grieved, and driven by her painful solicitude to acts that were indiscreet and unpleasant (Mark iii. 31; Matt. xii. 47). There is absolutely nothing here that argues that Mary did not know the incidents recorded by Matthew and Luke certainly nothing that has any weight compared with the positive reasons for believing that Mary was herself the authority upon which Luke based his story."

Further, the story of the Wedding at Cana (John ii. 3-5), which is no doubt based upon authentic tradition, implies an attitude of expectation on the part of Mary that her Son would be likely to do something wonderful her hopes had not yet been dashed by the unhappy conflict with the Scribes and Pharisees. There was nothing in the previous years of uneventful life at Nazareth to justify such evident Messianic expectations; but the remembrance of the wonderful events of the Birth may well have done so when Jesus had just begun His public ministry.

The evidence of the Fourth Gospel in relation to Our Lord's birth has been differently interpreted. Schmiedel states the case as follows ---

"Jesus in this Gospel says a great deal not only about his previous existence with God, but also about his entrance into this earthly life in virtue of his mission by his Father. In this connexion it would assuredly have been of great importance to have been able to say, in support of his exalted dignity, that he had been born in an altogether exceptional way. Instead of this, what do we find? That in John i. 45, Philip, in vi. 42, the Jews 2 call him the son of Joseph, that in i. 45 (Jesus of Nazareth), vii. 41 f. (Doth the Christ come out of Galilee? Hath not the Scripture said that the Christ cometh of the seed

of David, and from Bethlehem the village where David was, vii. 52 (Search and see that out of Galilee arise no prophet], Nazareth is spoken of as his birthplace, whilst yet Bethlehem is said to be of necessity the birthplace of the Messiah; and Jesus says nothing to the contrary. It is acknowledged that in the Fourth Gospel the objections of the Jews against Jesus continually proceed upon misunderstandings. But here the misunderstanding plainly lies not in any error as to the actual birthplace of Jesus or as to the manner of his birth, but only in the opinion that these facts exclude the Messiahship of Jesus."

This is a style of criticism against which it is necessary to enter a protest. It may be described as a form of hyper-criticism which is itself uncritical. If the writer of the Fourth Gospel had written in the way Schmiedel thinks he ought to have written, and had put into the mouth of Jesus assertions "that he had been born in an altogether exceptional way," he would at once have branded his work as an unhistorical romance. Because he did not commit himself to so palpable a fiction, we are asked to believe that he did not accept the Virgin Birth as a fact! We are also assured that in the Fourth Gospel "Nazareth is spoken of as his (Jesus) birthplace." Not one of the passages adduced supports this assertion. In fact, not a single passage in the New Testament categorically states that Nazareth was Jesus birthplace. Jesus is spoken of as "the Nazarene" and as "Coming from Galilee" which statements are, of course, historically true and it is a mere inference from such expressions to assume that He was born in Galilee. No doubt, the Jews were unaware that He had been born at Bethlehem; but the readers of the Fourth Gospel were certainly not. And when the Evangelist quotes the Jews as objecting, Hath not the Scripture said that the Christ cometh of the seed of David, and from Bethlehem the village where David was he is merely indulging, after his manner, in a species of tragic irony.

As I have said elsewhere ---

"It would be strange indeed if the writer of the Fourth Gospel possessed no knowledge of the tradition of the Virgin Birth of Jesus as embodied in Matt. i.-ii., and Luke i.-ii. Silence in this case would presumably imply not ignorance but tacit acceptance. Unless the traditions were contradicted either explicitly or tacitly, the presumption in such a case is that it was accepted. It is certainly significant that the Prologue to the Fourth Gospel, which occupies a similar place to that of the Genealogy in the First Gospel, traces the origin of the Logos which became incarnate in Christ to the inner life of God. What the genealogists attempted to do partially is here carried out fundamentally and finally. The question arises, Is the Prologue intended to be a tacit correction of the Matthaean and Lukan nativity-traditions? Or are these, at any rate as regards their central feature the Virgin Birth silently accepted and supplemented by the statement of fuller and deeper truth? The latter alternative accords with the characteristic manner and method of the Fourth Evangelist. So far from excluding the possibility of the Virgin Birth, it may be argued that the Prologue presupposes it. In view of the fact that the tradition of the Virgin Birth must already have been current in certain Christian circles, and can hardly have been unknown to the writer of the Johannine Prologue, this conclusion becomes at least highly probable. If the writer had conceived of the method of the Incarnation of the pre-existent Logos as being otherwise, we should at least have expected to find some hint or suggestion to that effect. In the only verse, however, in the Prologue where any allusion to birth occurs (John i. 13), the reference is certainly not incompatible with the tradition of the Virgin Birth, but may be regarded as lending it, if anything, some presumptive support."

The passage of the Prologue just referred to is worth a closer examination. It runs (John i. 12-14) as follows ----

(12) But as many as received him, to them gave he the right to become children of God, even to them that believe on his name; (13) which were born not of blood, nor of the will of the

flesh, nor of the will of man, but of God. (14) And the Word became flesh, and dwelt among us (and we beheld his glory a of the only begotten (povoyevovs) of the Father full of grace and truth. Carr (Exp. T. xviii. 522, 1907), contends that povoyevovs in v. 14, "from its position in the Prologue, and from its form as a composite of must refer not to the eternal generation of the Son of God, but to the human birth of the Son of Man." There is also the remarkable reading, known to Justin, Irenaeus, Tertullian, and perhaps Hippolytus, according to which v. 13 directly refers to Christ's supernatural birth: who (sing.) was born not of blood, nor of the will of the flesh, nor of the will of man, but of God. Here, natural generation by a human father is denied and excluded in the most categorical manner. Even if this reading be not accepted, it is a pertinent question to ask:

"Why the elaboration of the theme, above all why the flexaro? (will of man), unless he (the writer of the Prologue) has in mind the supernatural birth of the Logos as a kind of pattern or model of the birth of the children of God? As He was born into the world by supernatural conception, not through the process of human generation, so they were born out of the world into the higher life by a spiritual process, symbolized indeed by generation, but transcending it."

Another point to be remembered is this. Behind the Fourth Gospel, as behind the Synoptists, there lies a background of controversy. The writers are interested in maintaining certain truths which were the object of attack when they wrote. St. Matthew's Nativity-Narrative, as has already been pointed out, is dominated by apologetic motives of this kind. But by the time when the Fourth Gospel was written ---

"the miraculous birth was simply an item in a larger controversy. No one denied the miraculous birth except as an item in a larger denial. The controversy in which John was absorbed concerned the reality of the Incarnation. There was no controversy as to the Virgin Birth considered in itself. No one who accepted the Incarnation denied or thought of denying the miraculous birth. All who accepted the Incarnation accepted, as a matter of course, the miraculous birth. When, therefore, John wrote the sentence, The Word became flesh, he gave in his allegiance to that entire systematic interpretation of Christ with which, in the mind of the early Church, the miraculous birth was essentially bound up."

We have already seen how precarious the argument from silence is in the case of the Second and Fourth Gospels; and this applies, with even stronger force, to St. Paul's letters. Dr. Headlam rightly insists that ----

"his letters were in all cases occasional documents. They assume the ordinary Christian preaching and the ordinary knowledge of the Gospel history. They were not written to provide future ages with a complete idea of what Christianity was, and in a sense it must be considered accidental that any particular point of early Christianity is found in them. Supposing that 1 Corinthians had not survived, it would have been the customary thing to argue that S. Paul knew nothing at all about the Lord's Supper. S. Paul's Christological doctrine was of such a character that it would be natural for him to believe that Our Lord was born in a remarkable manner."

No stress can properly be laid either way on such phrases as born of a woman, born under the Law (Gal. iv. 4); born of the seed of David according to the flesh (Rom. i. 3). As the First Gospel most emphatically affirms the two propositions: (a) that Jesus belonged to the family of David, and (b) that He was virgin-born; it is obvious that such a phrase may include belief in the Virgin Birth. In any case, it cannot be insisted upon either for or against the belief. What is more important is St. Paul's doctrine of the Second Adam from heaven as applied to Christ. As has already been pointed out, there seems to be a real link of connexion between this doctrine and the Lukan genealogy, which traces the genealogical line of Our Lord back to Adam (Son) of God. The thought seems to be that just as the first Adam was Son of God by a direct creative act, without the intervention of a human father, so the Second Adam was created by the direct intervention of God, through a human mother it is true and, therefore, He was truly human (cf. Gal. iv. 4, "made of a woman") but without the intervention of a human father. That such a conception should be embodied in the Lukan genealogy is significant. Whence did St. Luke derive it if not from St. Paul? He was St. Paul's companion and disciple. If the disciple used this doctrine in connexion with the Virgin Birth, it is hard to believe that the master was ignorant of the latter. The most that can be urged is that in the Pauline Christology no emphasis was laid on the dogma of the Virgin Birth.

The obviously mythological figure in Rev. xii of the woman "arrayed with the sun" who "was delivered of a son," if it is derived from an earlier Jewish source, shows that the Babylonian myth was not unfamiliar among Apocalyptic circles within Judaism. It can hardly, however, have influenced or suggested the Jewish-Christian tradition of the Virgin Birth. "But," to use Mr. Allen's words, "it is worth while raising the question whether the author of the book (of Revelation) did not incorporate this section with direct reference to the tradition of the supernatural birth of Christ, with which he must, therefore, have been acquainted." This passage may, however, be left conveniently for discussion in the next chapter.

II

It is significant that the assertion of the fact of the Virgin Birth appeared in the earliest form of the Roman Creed: Who was born of the Holy Ghost from the Virgin Mary. This early form of the Western Creed is placed by Kattenbusch as far back as the year A.D. 100, and in any case is not much later. St. Ignatius (martyred between the years A.D. 107 and 116) writes early in the second century to the Ephesians as follows ---

For our God, Jesus the Christ was conceived in the womb by Mary according to a dispensation, of the seed of David but also of the Holy Ghost; and He was born and was baptized that by His passion He might cleanse water. And hidden from the prince of this world were the virginity of Mary and her childbearing and likewise also the death of the Lord three mysteries to be cried aloud which were wrought in the silence of God. (ad. Ephes. xviii. 19.)

It is noteworthy that the Ignatian Letters show no trace of the influence of the amplified Infancy-Narratives embodied in the Apocryphal Gospels; the writer apparently depends upon the birth narrative of the First Gospel, or something very much like it, and is acquainted with teaching similar in type to that of the Prologue of the Fourth Gospel. The pre-existent Word of God became incarnate through a human and virginal birth. Another early second-century witness to the Virgin Birth is the Apologist Aristides, a Syriac version of whose work was discovered in 1889. The Apology was addressed, according to the Syriac version, to the Roman Emperor Antoninus Pius (A.D. 138-161). In chapter ii the following occurs -----

The Christians, then, reckon the beginning of their religion from Jesus the Messiah, and He is named the Son of God Most High; and it is said that God came down from heaven, and from a Hebrew virgin took and clothed Himself with flesh, and in a daughter of man there dwelt the Son of God. This is taught in the Gospel, as it is called, which a short while ago was preached among them.

Another famous second-century Apologist, Justin Martyr, refers at length to the Virgin Birth in the Apology and in The Dialogue with Trypho; and the doctrinal fact is emphasized also v by Irenaeus, Hippolytus, and Tertullian, not to speak of later writers. It is thus clear that, to borrow Harnack's words, "by the middle or probably soon after the beginning of the second century this belief had become an established part of the Church tradition." As against Jew and Ebionite, on the one side, it was adduced to prove Our Lord's divine origin, and, on the other, against the Gnostic, to safeguard His true humanity. It is a striking fact that the Virgin Birth is a well-established part of the Christian tradition as far back as we can trace it, and was embedded in the earliest form of the Church's creeds. It was accepted by the great mass of the heretics, as well as by the orthodox. Nobody of tradition was ever more cautious and conservative than the authoritative tradition of the Church. That the assertion of the Virgin Birth of Our Lord is so firmly entrenched in this citadel, points unmistakably to the fact that it came to the Church, on its first publication, with the highest possible credentials and authority, and, in consequence, was at once accepted, though it had formed no part of the original Apostolic preaching.

CHAPTER VIII.THE ALLEGED PARALLELS FROM HEATHEN SOURCES

As early as the time of Justin Martyr (Trypho, I xvii) the mythological tales of virgin birth were cited to discredit the Christian doctrine. "Amongst the Grecian fables," says Trypho, "it is asserted that Perseus was born of the virgin Danae; Jupiter, as they call him, coming down upon her in a shower of gold." Such tales are widespread. "We can no longer ignore the fact," says Mr. Estlin Carpenter, "that the idea of a wondrous birth without human fatherhood appears in a multitude of tales which can be traced literally round the world from China to Peru." A large collection of these has been made in Hartland's Legend of Perseus. Students of comparative religion are sometimes apt to exaggerate resemblances which are small and to ignore profound and far-reaching differences. A comparison of the stories of virgin birth adduced from heathen sources serves to reveal how utterly unlike the Gospel-Narrative, both in form and spirit, these stories are. They belong to different worlds of thought and feeling. Thus, the legend of Perseus bears not the least resemblance to anything recorded of the birth and life of Jesus. Justin, in answer to Trypho, who brought forward the myth of Perseus as a heathen parallel to the story of the Virgin Birth of Our Lord, indignantly repudiates both the similarity and the connexion. "The Christian story is to him, he replies in substance, not only de facto historical and true in its essential points (while the pagan myths are mere Satanic counter feits of it), but . . . the two stories differ toto coelo morally and spiritually." In fact, the idea of a direct borrowing from Greek myth has largely been abandoned even by scholars who reject the story of Jesus miraculous birth. Some link more closely connected with the historical antecedents must be found. Another hypothesis seeks to explain the Gospel-story by a comparison with the Greek fables which impute the physical origin of great men (heroes and benefactors) to the gods (not only to Zeus, but to Apollo, Mars, Mercury), and which doubtless are the expression of popular feeling that finds in splendid endowments and achievements something marvelous and inexplicable, on purely natural grounds. The soil for such beliefs in the popular feeling and consciousness of the pagan world was a fertile one. But this was far from being the case among the Jews, at any rate within historical times, and it is difficult to see how such ideas about the sons of the gods could have found entrance into primitive Christian circles least of all, Jewish Christian circles. If the feeling had operated within Christian or Jewish circles why were not the Apostles turned into demi-gods, and why was not a divine origin ascribed to such mighty figures as Moses and Elijah? Soltau, however, finds no difficulty in adducing as parallels to the Gospel-story the fables circulated by Alexander (alleged to be a son of Zeus) and the Emperor Augustus as to their divine origin. Augustus, we are told, availing himself of a popular superstition, especially rife among the Romans, which regarded the serpent as "the symbol of the Genius, the protecting spirit of the family---"

"caused sacrifices to be offered everywhere to the Genius of the Emperor; (and) he was careful that the fable should be widely diffused, to the effect that his mother Atia was once, while asleep in the temple of Apollo, visited by the god in the form of a serpent, and that in the tenth month afterwards he himself was born."

"Was it to be wondered at, then, that kindred ideas grew up with regard to the origin of Christ also, and that they found credence? This, at any rate, is clear; the belief in the Virgin Birth of Jesus could not have originated in Palestine; anyhow it could never have taken its rise in Jewish circles."

As we have already seen that nothing is more certain than the Jewish-Christian origin and character of the Gospel Nativity-Narratives, we need not here do more than endorse Harnack's verdict that "the conjecture that the idea of a birth from a virgin is a heathen myth, which was received by Christians, contradicts the entire earliest development of Christian tradition." Nor need we linger over the parallel derived from the story of the birth of the Buddha, which is as remote from any resemblance to the Gospel-story as can well be imagined. It is thus described ---

His mother before the conception retires to keep the fast, and in complete chastity sleeps surrounded by her women. Her husband is not there. As she sleeps she dreams a dream; it seems as if a white elephant enters her side. This is the conception.

It should be noted that there is no suggestion here that the mother was a virgin at the time. The more careful exponents of the scholarship which seeks to explain the Gospel-Narratives from the side of comparative religion see clearly that direct borrowing from heathen sources is out of the question. This group of scholars, which includes not only Gunkel and Gressmann but also Cheyne, insists on the Jewish-Christian character of the Gospel-Narratives. It is assumed that a folk-lore motif had already penetrated Jewish circles before the Christian period, and that a Jewish legend really a heathen myth transformed and invested with a Jewish character had grown up about the Messiah. The most recent exposition of this kind of treatment is that of Gressmann, which may here be examined.

As we have already seen, Gressmann holds that the Gospel "legend" simply reflects a Jewish birth-legend of the Messiah which was dominated by the foundling motif. Whence was this derived? The foundling motif is very common in folk-tales, sagas, and myths. One version of it, "which in a striking way approximates to the Christmas gospel," is extant in Plutarch s Isis and Osiris, Chapter xii: "which is particularly valuable for our purpose, because Plutarch is a contemporary of the Evangelists and therefore cannot be dependent upon them." Plutarch is aware of the celebration of the birth festivals of Egyptian gods on the intercalary days at the end of the year, and in particular gives an account of the birth of Osiris: On the first (intercalary) day Osiris is born. Coincident with the birth a voice resounded from the (heavenly) height: "The Lord of all emerges into the light." Some, however, assert that a certain Pamyles in Thebes, while drawing water from the Temple of Zeus, heard a voice which commanded him to proclaim aloud: "The great King, the Benefactor, Osiris, is born." And when Kronos handed him (Osiris) over to him, he brought up Osiris, and therefore the Feast of Pamyles was celebrated in his honor, which is similar to the Phallus-feasts. Here, Plutarch sets before us two variations of the birth-legend of Osiris, the second of which is rather fuller. The situation implied is that the divine child is born in a marvelous manner. Then suddenly a heavenly voice sounds from the Temple of Zeus-Amon (according to the first account, from the heavenly height), and announces the birth, giving direction, at the same time, that the fact should be proclaimed, so that everyone's attention should be called to the matter. Pamyles, who was occupied in drawing water a task only allotted to slaves or servants of the lower order can have been no priest. When, in his astonishment, he looks about, he becomes aware of the child's presence. He does not for one moment doubt that Kronos-Geb, the father of Osiris, has entrusted him with the care of the child. So he brings him up as his own, and announces the theophany that has been vouchsafed to him. The place where this happened is not expressly mentioned; Gressmann thinks it must have been on the banks of the Nile, near which the Theban Temple lay. The legend probably has as its foundation was the idea of a foundling set by the water. The differences between this legend and the assumed Messiah-legend are admitted to be formidable. This is accounted for (1) by the difference of background; in the Theban river country it must be a drawer of water who lights on the foundling, while in the hill-country of Bethlehem, it is shepherds to whom this role must be assigned, and who find the child in a cave; (2) another difference is that in the Gospel-legend the infant is found wrapped in swaddling-clothes (cf. also Ezek. xvi. 4), a custom which, apparently, was unknown to the Egyptians.

In both accounts the heavenly command is taken up by the recipients, who are in each case poor people of the lower orders, in Plutarch a water-drawer, in St. Luke shepherds. The legend of Plutarch, it is claimed, confirms the analysis of the Lukan story by which an older form of the Messiah-legend is detected that narrates the wonderful birth of the Christ-child suddenly, with out parents, in solitude far from human society and helpless, in a manger. But, by the coincident announcement of the angel, the shepherds who are in the open country, are informed of the event, and proceed to the manger. Since they know that the child is of divine origin and destined for great things, they not only make the divine announcement known, but take charge of the babe, give him milk to drink, and bring him up.

It will be noticed that the basis of comparison here with the Osiris-legend is a hypothetically reconstructed pre-Christian Jewish one. Not a particle of positive evidence is adduced for the existence of such a legend. In particular, the foundling idea is far to seek. If anything is fixed in Jewish popular notions about the Messiah, it is that he is to be born of a human mother who is known as such. This is as clear as it can possibly be in the Jewish legend of the birth of the Messiah which has already been quoted. Another condition which must have controlled any local tradition about Messiah's birth that may have grown up at Bethlehem is that the future King must be a scion of the House of David, that is to say, his father must be known to belong to the Davidic family. Otherwise, why should Bethlehem be the scene of his birth? In the light of these objections, it seems to us that the possibility of the growth, in such a connexion, of a foundling-legend vanishes. Attempts have also been made to connect the birth-story of Jesus with the Mithraic birth-legend. The resemblance in certain respects between the religion of Mithra and of Christ was sufficiently striking to impress so early a Christian Father as Justin, who (Trypho, ch. I xx) refers to the matter as follows ---

And when they who treat of the mysteries of Mithra say that he sprang from a rock, and call that place, where they say those that believe in him are initiated by him a cave, is it not certain that they have imitated that which was spoken by Daniel, that a stone was cut out of a great mountain without hands (Dan. ii. 34)? And likewise that which is spoken by Isaiah (Is. xxxiii 13-20), all whose words they have endeavored to imitate as exactly as possible? For the evil spirits have contrived to have the precepts concerning the practice of that which is just and right taught even by the priests of Mithra.

Again, in ch. I xxviii, Justin refers definitely to the caves of Mithra in speaking of the cave at Bethlehem where Our Lord, according to him, was born. The god Mithra, as is well known, was worshipped in caves or artificially made cave chapels, and was spoken of as the "rock-born." It is difficult, however, to believe that a cave-chapel of Mithra existed near Bethlehem at so early a period as the first century B.C. The evidence does not suggest that the Mithra-cult was known in Syria till a long time subsequently. Yet the hypothesis apparently requires that we must assume the existence of a cave near Bethlehem, sacred to Mithra at a very early period; and that this was taken over into Jewish-Christian legend. This is incredible. Nor is an indirect influence of such a legend any more probable.

Cheyne working on different lines has made out a much stronger case for the introduction of mythical material into the Christian birth-stories. He emphatically rejects the view that the statement of Christ's Virgin Birth originated in a mistranslation of the Immanuel-prophecy (Is. vii. 14), or in a non-Jewish, heathen story, adopted by Gentile Christians a story such as those which Mr. Hartland in his Perseus and Prof. Usener in his Weihnachts fest have collected in abundance. The influence he postulates is, rather, Babylonian, and he discovers traces of it in the mythological figure of "the woman clothed with the sun" of Rev. xii, who seems to be regarded by the author of the passage as the mother of the Messiah.

He calls attention to the fact that "this strange and difficult narrative" (i.e., Rev. xii) ---

"makes no reference to the Messiah's father. This may be explained by the hypothesis that in the Oriental myth upon which this Jewish narrative is based, the mother alone was mentioned. For the woman clothed with the sun evidently represents one of those heathen goddesses (e.g., Istar, Isis, Artemis) who were mothers, but not originally wives in short virgins, in the sense in which Trapivos was applied to the great mother-goddess of Asia Minor. It appears probable that in some of the early Jewish versions of the Oriental myth of the Divine Redeemer (which has not, so far as we know as yet, been preserved) the mother of the Holy Child was called a virgin for nothing is easier than for divine titles to pass from one religion to another, and for their original meaning to be forgotten. In other versions it is possible that the title adopted was the woman, a term which may be directly traceable to Babylonia. For the former title we can with some confidence refer to the Septuagint rendering of ha-alma in Is. vii. 14 (nirapdevos, whence the rendering in our version), which I know not how otherwise to explain, than as an allusion to a belief current among the translators contemporaries, and for the latter to Rev. xii (by implication), and just possibly to a passage in the (Ethiopic) Book of Enoch (I xix 29), where the oldest manuscript has, not Son of man, but Son of woman."

Prof. Cheyne fortifies his hypothesis by another reference drawn from Babylonian literature. He cites the remarkable traditional story of the Babylonian King Sargon of Agade, who flourished about 3800 B.C.

"It is a legend of mythic origin, and represents the great king as having been born of a poor mother in secret, and as not knowing his father. There is reason to suspect that something similar was originally said by the Israelites of Moses, and would it be strange if a similar account were given of the birth of Jesus Christ, the second Moses?"

In criticizing this theory, I may, perhaps, be allowed to repeat what I have said elsewhere

----

"It is undoubtedly true that the Jewish Messianic idea bears traces of the influence of the universal myth of the World Redeemer. It is, indeed, when analyzed critically, found to be largely a transformed and refined edition of the old material. The universal craving which found varying expression in the world-myth of the coming Deliverer assumed its highest and most spiritual phase in some forms of the Jewish Messianic belief. One feature of the widespread myth was the representation of the mother of the coming Deliverer. The mother plays an important role, but no father is mentioned. Here, in all probability, we must see a survival of the idea of the goddess-mother as distinct from the later one of the goddess-wife. In Is. vii 14, the goddess-mother, it would seem, has been transferred to earth, and has become simply the Israelitish woman who is to bear the wonderful child. The heathenish trappings have been entirely dropped."

As we have already seen, in Rabbinical literature this idea seems to have survived in the various forms in which the conception of the Messiah's earthly pre-existence comes to expression.

(1) He is represented as leading a hidden life and then suddenly manifests himself (cf. Mt. xxiv. 27, 43, 44; John vii. 27). In the Midrash Ex. Rabbd, i, it is said that as Moses, the first deliverer, was reared at the court of Pharaoh so the future Deliverer will grow up in the Roman capital. Another Midrash says that the Messiah will suddenly be revealed to Israel in Rome.

(2) The Messiah is represented as born, but not yet revealed; cf. the well-known passage, Sank. 98 b., where R. Joshua b. Lev! is quoted as saying that the Messiah is already born and is living in concealment at the gates of Rome. According to the Targ. (Jerus) on Mic. iv. 8, the Messiah is on the earth, but is still in concealment because of the sins of the people.

(3) The Messiah is represented as having been born at some time in the past (according to one account born at Bethlehem on the day the Temple was destroyed; according to another, born in the days of King David, and now dwelling at Rome).

In the curious story of the Messiah's birth quoted by Lightfoot (Home on Mt. ii) the birth of the Messiah (whose name is Menahem, son of Hezekiah) is connected with Bethlehem and the destruction of the Temple. His mother's name is not given, she being described simply as "the mother of Menahem." At Bethlehem she is found with her infant son by the Jew who has been mysteriously apprised of the Messiah's birth. The Jew leaves, and after some days returns to that city, and says to her, how does the little infant? And she said: "From the time you saw me last spirits and tempests came, and snatched him away out of my hands."

In all these forms of the myth, it is to be observed that the mother of the Redeemer is nowhere called a "virgin." Where the mention of a father does not occur, this feature may be due to the prominence of the mother in an earlier social stage, surviving in the form of the goddess-mother; an idea which later assumed the form of the Messiah's being concealed and unknown, and manifesting Himself suddenly. It is also to be observed that in Rev. xii the woman is a heavenly being; in other words, the conception in this passage is nearer the primitive myth than it is in Is. vii. 14. It is difficult to imagine how the representation in Rev. xii can have suggested the idea of the virgin birth, though it is easy to see that the prominence assigned to the Virgin-

Mother of Jesus in the Christian story may have influenced the author of Revelation in selecting so crude a piece of mythological material for the purposes of his book. In other words, it was the Gospel story which suggested the selection of the mythical representation in Rev. xii. It would be easier to suppose that the LXX. of Is. vii. 14 had given rise to the story of the Virgin Birth than the mythical figure in Revelation.

In order to overcome this difficulty, Prof. Cheyne is driven to conjecture "that in some of the early Jewish versions of the Oriental myth of the Divine Redeemer (which has not, so far as we know as yet, been preserved) the mother of the Holy Child was called a virgin." And, further, it is necessary to suppose that Trapivos ("virgin"), which in its original application (e.g., to the great mother goddess of Asia Minor) meant one who was not bound by the marriage tie (and, therefore, connoted anything but the virginity of Lk. i. 34) in the process of transition to the conjectured Jewish version of the myth, lost its original connotation, and was interpreted in the strict sense; "for nothing is easier than for Divine titles to pass from one religion to another, and for their original meaning to be forgotten."

It is very difficult to believe that any "Jewish versions of the Oriental myth" ever existed which spoke of the Messiah s Mother as a "virgin." Virginity, in the strict sense of the term, was never esteemed among Jews proper as a higher state than marriage; nor do the Gospel Nativity-Stories suggest that such an idea had any influence in creating them. The home of Joseph, Mary, and Jesus, as pictured in these narratives, was a Jewish home, permeated with the atmosphere of conjugal love; the picture does not harmonize with an ascetic ideal of virginity. But the ascetic ideal of virginity is one thing; the idea of a virgin-mother is another. It is incredible that Jews can have taken over this idea from heathen sources, especially with such associations clinging to it as those described by Prof. Cheyne. That the very idea of a virgin-mother was abhorrent to Jews is reflected clearly in St. Matthew's narrative; and we have already seen that Jewish literature shows not the slightest trace of the idea of the Messiah's mother being a virgin. It is true that the LXX of Is. vii. describes the mother of the future Deliverer as a Trapievos ("virgin"). But there is no evidence that this text ever received a Messianic application among Jews, apart from Matt. i. 23; and there it was suggested by the event, and not vice verse. What, then, was the significance of the LXX Trapievos in Is. vii. 14 to Greek-speaking Jewish readers? Two explanations are possible: either (1) the translators, in using the term, intended to enhance the miraculous character of the sign, given by God Himself, as the prophet announced, to Ahaz contrary to all natural laws God Himself will bring it about that a virgin shall conceive and bear a son; or (2) it may simply mean (and this, perhaps, is more natural) that some definite person (known to Ahaz and the prophet), who is now a virgin, shall conceive, etc., the implication being that she will have ceased to be a virgin before the conception and birth of a son. In face of the silence of the entire Jewish literature apart from the Jewish-Christian narratives and the positive and negative evidence against the currency of such an idea it is surely precarious to see evidence in this isolated text of a belief, prevalent among the Jewish-Greek contemporaries of the LXX translators, in the Virgin Birth of the Messiah.

On the general question of heathen analogies to the Virgin Birth of Our Lord, it should not be forgotten that, while many of these stories and myths can only be described as "the shameless glorifying of sensual desire," which "could only provoke in the primitive Christian consciousness the deepest abhorrence," yet, in some, a religious motive is discernible. This element seems to be present in the stories told of the birth of Egyptian kings. In the early period, the kings of the Fifth and Sixth Dynasties called themselves "sons" of the sun-god. In the case of Amon-Hotep III (of the Eighteenth Dynasty) we are told that the god Amon himself descended from heaven and stood beside the virgin who should become a mother ---

"Amon-Hotep," he is made to say, "is the name of the son who is in thy womb. He shall grow up according to the words that proceed out of thy mouth. He shall exercise sovereignty and righteousness in this land unto its very end. My soul is in him (and) he shall wear the twofold crown of royalty, ruling the two worlds like the sun forever."

"This," says Dr. J. Estlin Carpenter, "is only the natural sequel of the language in which again and again the Egyptian kings are described as filially related to a paternal god." On the whole question, some weighty words of Professor Sanday may well be pondered.

"If we believe that the course of human ideas, however mixed in their character as all human things are mixed is yet part of a single development, and that development presided over by a Providence which at once imparts to it unity and prescribes its goal those who believe this may well see in the fantastic outgrowth of myth and legend something not wholly undesigned or wholly unconnected with the Great Event which was to be, but rather a dim unconscious preparation for that Event, a groping towards it of the human spirit, a prophetic instinct gradually molding the forms of thought in which it was to find expression."

It is, however, all-important to remember that the Gospel-Narratives belong to the sphere of history, and were produced under the limitations that condition the record of historic facts. The creations of the mythopoeic fancy flourish in a different atmosphere. "They are part of a common stock of imaginative material reproduced without purpose or authority from age to age and land to land, destitute of historic significance."

A careful student, after a survey of the whole question, sums up as follows: "After a laborious and occasionally wearisome study of the evidence offered and the analogies urged," he says, he is "convinced that heathenism knows nothing of virgin births. Supernatural births it has without number, but never from a virgin in the New Testament sense and never without physical generation, except in a few isolated instances of magical births on the part of women who had not the slightest claim to be called virgins." In all recorded instances, so far as the writer has been able to examine them, "if the mother was a virgin before conception took place, she could not make that claim afterwards. The supernatural conception of Christ, therefore, was unique in several particulars: (1) Christ's conception was in order to incarnation heathen wonder-births were the result of incarnation. (2) The story combines a miraculous birth with a pure spiritualistic monotheism. Christ's birth was due to the creative agency of the unseen God without the usual human mediation. (3) His mother was at the time of His conception and remained until after His birth a virgin. In short, the conception of Jesus was as unique as the person thus brought into the world."

CHAPTER IX.CONCLUSION

We are now in a position to sum up the conclusions that have been reached in the previous chapters, and to attempt, briefly, to estimate their religious significance.

(1) The Historic Fact

If the account that has been given of the character and genesis of these narratives be even approximately correct, what room is left for the operation within them of heathen superstitious ideas? How ever much Jews at various times have been influenced by their pagan neighbors, in the sphere of religion, and especially in their conceptions of God, they are the last persons ever to have been affected by pagan superstitions. Towards such, and towards all the associations of idolatry in all its forms, they took small pains to disguise their aversion and contempt, as witness the Maccabean revolt and the conflicts with the Roman Government on the question of worship of the Emperors.

Yet we are asked by Soltau to believe that "the idea of the supernatural descent of Augustus" (embodied in the fable that his mother, while asleep in the Temple of Apollo, was visited by the God in the form of a serpent, and later gave birth to Augustus) was "applied to the case of Jesus." Soltau, indeed, concedes that "the belief in the Virgin Birth of Jesus could not have originated in Palestine; anyhow it could never have taken its rise in Jewish circles" and in this view he is supported by Schmiedel and Usener. Consequently he is driven to regard the story of the Virgin Birth as an "insertion" in the original narrative, of "Hellenistic origin." The difficulties that beset this theory of "insertion" have already been indicated. How is it that such "insertions" should have taken so characteristic a Jewish form? This, at any rate, must be the work of Jews. Moreover, why should such alien elements have crystallized themselves in just the most markedly Jewish parts of the New Testament, while they are passed over in silence elsewhere?

Gunkel, indeed, fully admits the Jewish-Christian character of the whole of the narrative of St. Luke, and boldly argues that the idea of the Virgin Birth of the Messiah must have become a Christological dogma in Jewish circles before the time of Jesus, in the same way as the Messiah's birth at Bethlehem and of the family of David had become a fixed popular Jewish belief; and that this was transferred to the history of Jesus. But, in support of this statement, not a scrap of positive evidence is given. If such were the case, why is the Virgin Birth of the Messiah never alluded to in the main body of the Gospels in connexion with the other popular beliefs (such as his birth at Bethlehem and of the family of David) that are mentioned? In fact, so far from it being a popular or even familiar belief among the Jews, it may be inferred with practical certainty from St. Matthew's narrative that the story of the Virgin Birth was a stumbling-block to Jewish readers which it required special apologetic efforts to overcome. The natural and instinctive Jewish attitude towards such a story was represented by a section of the later Ebionites, who, while admitting other claims on behalf of Jesus, refused to believe this. Nor can it be said that either Gressmann's or Cheyne's attempt to postulate a pre-Christian Jewish birth legend of the Messiah which would account for the New Testament Nativity-Narratives has been successful.

The conclusion is forced upon us, therefore, that if the story of the Virgin Birth is a legend, it must have grown up within the Jewish-Christian community of Palestine, and must represent a primitive Christological dogma expressing the idea of the perfect moral and spiritual purity of Jesus as Son of God. The Christian consciousness, it might be urged, working on such a passage as Thou art my Son; this day have I begotten Thee (Ps. ii. 7), together with the Scriptural promise of the fullness of the spirit that should rest upon the Messiah (Is. xi. 2), may have been led to transfer these ideas to the physical beginnings of Jesus life. But, in the absence of any analogous development in the Christian consciousness elsewhere this is hard to believe. Why did the Christological process assume just this form and in this (a priori most unlikely) quarter? The impulse must have been given from without. But, unless the idea came from heathen sources which to us seems inconceivable in so strictly Jewish a circle then it must have grown out of a conviction, cherished at first within a limited Palestinian circle of believers, that the traditional belief among them was based upon facts of which some members of this community had been the original depositories and witnesses.

Dr. Estlin Carpenter agrees with Lobstein in thinking that the story of Our Lord's Virgin Birth is a pious creation of "early Christian imagination." We have already seen how the pious Christian imagination works in our study of the Apocryphal Gospels. "These show," says Dr. Plummer, "what pitiful stuff the imagination of early Christians could produce, even when the canonical Gospels were there as their models. All these classes of fiction (both heathen and Christian) warn us that we must seek some other source for the Gospel-Narrative other than the fertile imagination of some Gentile or Jewish Christian whose curiosity led him to speculate upon a mysterious subject. We should have had something very different, both in details and in tone, if there had been no better source than this."

When subjected to the criteria properly applicable to it and when weighed in the light of the considerations advanced above such a tradition, it seems to us, has high claims to historical credibility. The alternative explanations only serve to raise more difficulties than they profess to solve.

Assuming, then, the historic fact of the Virgin Birth, and frankly accepting its "miraculous" character, we are not thereby driven to suppose that the miracle is incongruous with the laws of nature. The essential truth embodied in the Christian tradition has been admirably stated by Professor Briggs ----

"The virgin conception of Jesus is not to be interpreted as if it were a miracle in violation of the laws of nature, but rather as brought about by God Himself present in theophany. The conception of Jesus in the womb of the Virgin Mary differs from all other conceptions of children by their mothers in that there was no human father. The place of the human father was taken by God Himself; not that God appeared in theophany in human form to beget the child, after the analogy of the mythologies of the ethnic religions, but that God in a theophany in an extraordinary way, unrevealed to us, impregnates the Virgin Mary with the holy seed. The words of the angel imply a theophanic presence; for though it might be urged that the coming of the Spirit upon her was an invisible coming, after the analogy of many passages of the Old Testament, yet the parallel statement that the Divine power overshadowed her cannot be so interpreted. For it not only in itself represents that the Divine power covered her with a shadow, but this is to be thought of, after the uniform usage of Scripture, as a bright cloud of glory, hovering over her, resting upon her, enveloping her with a halo of Divinity, in the moment when the Divine energy enabled her to conceive the child Jesus."

On the view that the narratives embody authentic history, it is obvious that they must either directly or indirectly depend upon the authority of Joseph and Mary themselves. And this is confirmed by their general character. It has often been noted that the narrative in the First Gospel is written from the point of view of Joseph, while St. Luke's reflects that of Mary. This is a very striking feature, and it is extraordinarily difficult to suppose that it is the result of invention or pure imagination. Especially so in the case of St. Luke's narrative. As Dr. Plummer remarks ----

"It required more delicacy to tell the story of the Virgin Birth from Mary's side than from Joseph's; and this .greater delicacy is forth coming. And it is all the more conspicuous because St. Luke s narrative is the richer in details. We conclude, therefore, that St. Luke has good authority for what he has told us, viz., an authority well acquainted with the facts. For if he was incapable of imagining what he has related, equally incapable was his informant. The narrative which he has handed on to us is what it is because in the main it sets forth what is true."

St. Luke's narrative may have been derived directly from Mary herself, or, more probably, from a document which depends ultimately upon the authority of the Virgin. Many scholars have pointed out the touches of a woman's hand in the narrative. "The notes of time (Luke i. 26, 36, 56) are specially feminine." Dr. Sanday indeed has argued that the narrative came not only from a woman, but through a woman, and has suggested, that Joanna, the wife of Chuza steward to Herod Antipas (Luke viii. 2-3, xxiv. 10; cf. xxiii. 49, and Acts i. 14), may have been the person through whom the information passed from Mary to St. Luke. It is quite possible that St. Luke received information orally from such a person, and that it formed the basis of the prose setting in which are embedded the poems of the Nativity. These poems, however, cannot have been composed by St. Luke. As has been argued in Chapter III, they are to be regarded as translations from Hebrew originals. We may confidently accept Dr. Briggs verdict, who says (New Light): "Making every allowance for the poetic form, style, and conception, these poems are sources of the highest value, and of the first degree of historic importance. They give us information as to the Infancy of Jesus Christ and as to the Virgin Mother, which is necessary to complete the story of their lives and to give us a complete understanding of their character."' Dr. Briggs detects seven pieces y of poetry in the Lukan narrative, none of which is, he thinks, in its present form complete. They are in the nature of incomplete extracts.

These poems are: (1) The Annunciation to Zacharias (Luke i. 13-17), a trimeter poem, in the original Hebrew, in two strophes of different lengths, evidently incomplete in the translation; (2) the Annunciation to Mary (Luke i. 28, 30-33, 35-37, 38), four pieces of trimeter poetry of different lengths, also incomplete; (3) the Annunciation to the Shepherds (Luke ii. 10-12, 14), two pieces of trimeter poetry, evidently extracts; (4) the Song of Elizabeth (Luke i. 42-45), and (5) the Song of the Virgin (the Magnificat) (Luke i. 46-55), both trimeter poems, perhaps also incomplete; (6) the Song of Zacharias (the Benedictus) Luke i. 68-79), a pentameter poem in two strophes, probably, relatively, the most complete of all, but, perhaps, an extract; and (7) the Song of Simeon (Nunc Dimittis) (Luke ii. 29-32, 34-35), a trimeter poem, probably incomplete.

It will be noticed that six of these seven pieces are of the same form (trimeter poems), while one (the Benedictus) is in pentameter form, which agrees with the extract in Matt. i. 20-21 (the Annunciation to Joseph). May these extracts go back to two long poems, one written in trimeter, the other in pentameter form, each giving a poetic account of the Birth of the Baptist and the Birth and Infancy of Jesus? We cannot say. At any rate, it seems clear that these poems were before St. Luke in written form when he wrote his Nativity-Narrative. Their composition must have taken place well before the destruction of Jerusalem in A.D. 70, "either in the Christian congregation of Jerusalem, or the Christian community in Galilee, therefore by early Christian poets who had access to the family of Jesus, certainly to His brother James, the head of the Jerusalem Church, and possibly also to the Virgin-Mother and to others who could speak as eye-witnesses and ear-witnesses of (some of) these matters embodied in verse." When the contents of the poems are examined, we find that they reflect an early type of Messianic belief and; expectation, and a primitive Christology which point to a very early date. It is evident that they emanate from a circle which was deeply interested not only in Jesus but in the Baptist. We may infer, with some certainty that they grew up in the earliest generation of Jewish-Christians, who had largely been drawn from those who were originally followers of the Baptist. It was from these elements that the community was formed in which these poems must have first taken shape. We may fix, approximately, on the decade A.D. 40-50, as the time within which they first assumed literary shape. But it is evident, of course, that the tradition on which they are based is much older.

The poems breathe "the spirit of the Messianic hope before it had received the rude and crushing blow involved in the rejection of the Messiah." This is specially noteworthy in the poems which belong to the Baptist-cycle. The Forerunner is to make ready a people prepared for the Lord (Luke i. 17). God hath holpen His servant that He might remember mercy (as He spake unto our fathers) toward Abraham and his seed for ever (i. 54-55); He hath visited and wrought redemption for His people, And raised up a horn of salvation for us in the House of His servant David, As he spake by the mouth of the holy ones, His prophets of old Salvation from our enemies, and from the hand of all that hate us; To show mercy toward our Fathers and to remember His holy covenant; The oath which He sware unto Abraham, our father (i. 68-71). The same Messianic hope is also reflected in the other songs. The child is to have the throne of his father David, and is to reign over the house of Jacob for ever (i. 32-33). Now, this "is not the sort of language that early Jewish Christians would have invented after the rejection of Christ." It reflects the earlier type of Messianic hope of which we have already spoken. The early chapters of the Acts show us that the primitive Jerusalem Church still hoped and worked for the winning of the Jewish people as a whole to the acceptance of Jesus as the Messiah, and not without some prospects of success. It is in such an atmosphere that a little circle could have cherished the tradition of earlier Messianic hopes reflected in the stories of the Birth and Infancy of the Baptist and of Jesus. It is true that this cycle of tradition did not form part of the Apostolic preaching, which laid all the emphasis on the death and Resurrection of Our Lord. But, as we have already seen, the very idea of Apostleship limited the teaching given by the Apostles to matters on which they could give personal testimony as eye-witnesses. What it is more important to observe is that, as in the early chapters of the Acts, the conception of the person of Jesus in St. Luke's Nativity-Narrative is purely Messianic. He is to be great and shall be called the Son of the Highest (Luke i. 32); He is to be the exalted Messiah; "but the doctrine of the Incarnation, strictly speaking, is not more to be found here than in the early speeches of the Acts." The Church had not yet sounded the depths, or fully developed the implications of her doctrine of Christ's Person.

It has already been suggested that the poems may have been influenced by other Jewish models, that in some cases the diction may have been borrowed from formulas familiar to Jews and sanctioned by liturgical usage (cf, e.g., the affinities between the Raddish and the angelic song in the Annunciation to the Shepherds).

A feature of the Nativity-Narratives that creates difficulty for some minds and tends to discredit the Gospel accounts by investing them with an air of unreality is the angelic appearances. This question has been admirably discussed by Dr. Gore, who points out that "to suppose such angelic appearances to be imaginative outward representations of what were in fact real but merely inward communications of the divine word to human souls, is both a possible course and one which is quite consistent with accepting the narrative as substantially historical and true." The prophets who speak of the "word of the Lord" as "coming to them" imply by such language "the reality of substantive divine communications to man of a purely inward sort." Such an inward communication is recorded to have been made to Elizabeth (Luke i. 41-45); "and the angelic appearances to Joseph recorded by St. Matthew (Matt. i. 20, ii. 13, 19) are merely inward occurrences (i.e., they are intimations conveyed to his mind in sleep)." "No one who knows human nature can doubt that such inward communications could be easily transformed by the imagination into outward forms," and especially in poetry. Zacharias may have received, in answer to earnest prayer (Luke i. 15) such an inward divine intimation as to what was to befall him, especially on so solemn an occasion as that described by St. Luke; and this may easily "have represented itself to his imagination in the outward form and voice of an angel." And similar explanations may be given of Mary's vision and that of the Shepherds.

As we have seen, the evidence suggests that the secret of Jesus birth was not at first generally made known. There were obvious reasons why this should have been the case during the lifetime of the Virgin. Yet some of the facts which invested both the birth of the Baptist and of Jesus with such an extraordinary significance must have been known from the first to an inner circle. These facts and occurrences seem gradually to have crystallized themselves into the tradition embodied in the poems that are utilized in the Lukan narrative, which may not have assumed final literary shape (in the original Hebrew form) till the decade A. D. 40-50.

It has already been pointed out that in all probability, one strong motive at work in the Matthean account was to meet Jewish calumny regarding Jesus birth. This may have come to a head after the narrative embodied in St. Luke's Gospel had become known, though its beginnings may have been even earlier. If this view is correct, the Matthean narrative must have been composed later than the Lukan (though it depends upon a similar early cycle of tradition) which shows no such strong apologetic interest, and contains more original material.

(2) Doctrine and Fact

When we ask ourselves, what is the doctrinal significance of the fact, and what is its theological value? We are raising questions of special delicacy and difficulty, which are acutely felt by many Christians today. In some quarters, where the Incarnation is accepted as a fact, it is assumed as almost axiomatic that the Nativity-Narratives of the Gospels have been discredited by historical criticism, and may safely be rejected. It is also suggested that the alleged fact of the Virgin Birth of Jesus has no doctrinal value. In the present discussion, an attempt has been made, patiently and frankly, to test the historical credibility of the narratives, and we have deliberately come to the conclusion that the Gospel-story possesses high claims to historicity. The argument is addressed to those who accept the Incarnation as a fact. It cannot be expected that those who do not approach the narratives with the presuppositions involved in the orthodox Christian belief as to the Person of Christ will be convinced by the Gospel evidence. "The historical evidence for Our Lord's birth of a virgin," says Dr. Gore, "is in itself strong and cogent. But it is not such as to compel belief. There are ways to dissolve its force." Such ways, as we have seen, have been found by historical criticism in abundance; and this criticism has not been without effect even on devout believers in the Incarnation. To quote Dr. Gore again "to produce belief there is needed in this as in almost all other questions of historical fact besides cogent evidence, also a perception of the meaning and naturalness, under the circumstances, of the event to which evidence is borne. To clinch the historical evidence for Our Lord's Virgin Birth there is needed the sense that, being what He was, His human birth could hardly have been otherwise than is implied in the virginity of His mother."

The Doctrinal Value and Significance of the Fact

What is the doctrinal value and significance of the fact? To this question orthodox Christian theology has a quite definite answer. We may not be able to say that the Incarnation could only have happened in the way described in the Gospels (i.e., by Our Lord's birth from a Virgin-Mother). But we can say that such a way is congruous with the Church's belief in Our Lord's pre-existence as a Divine Person; that it safeguards at once His Divinity and His humanity, and also His uniqueness; and that there are grave difficulties in reconciling these positions of Christian theology with the theory of ordinary generation from two human parents.

Dr. Briggs has expressed the matter trenchantly as follows ---

"The Christ of the Bible and the Church is not merely a divinely inhabited man, but the God-man. The deity and the humanity are inseparable, and eternally united in one and the same divine person. Mary the virgin, the mother of Jesus, was the mother of God because she gave birth not simply to a man, but God who had become man in her womb when she conceived him by the Holy Ghost. Christ is not God in the sense that he is the elder brother of an indefinite number of other gods; but in the sense that he is, and always will be, the one only unique Son of the Father, the second person of the Holy Trinity. A birth by human generation would give us only an individual man, inhabited by the Son of God, and so two distinct persons, the second person of the Trinity, and the person of the man Jesus. That cannot in any way be reconciled with the faith of the Bible, or the Church. It is simply the revival of ancient errors rejected by the Church once for all and for ever nearly fifteen centuries ago."

With this, a statement by Dr. Bethune-Baker may be compared. He says ---

"I have frequently, as a student of Christian doctrine, been asked by devout believers in the Godhead of our Lord, to whom the belief in His miraculous Birth was a part of the accepted tradition which, as far as they knew, had no influence on their main belief, to tell them what place in the whole doctrine of the Incarnation I conceived that that particular miracle occupied; how the manner of His birth was related to the doctrine of His Person. To this question I have not been able to give many of the answers which have been given or suggested by great divines of the Church in the past. Some of the most familiar answers seem to me to be either essentially docetic, in failing to recognize adequately our Lord's full manhood, or based on biological conceptions which we know now were mistaken. I have only been able to answer to the effect that the doctrine as I understand it requires continuity with the human race, which is secured by birth from a woman heredity through the mother and at the same time a break in the continuity of the ordinary, natural process, a fresh departure, a new Divine action, the introduction of a new Power into the world, which is secured by conception, without human paternity, by the direct operation of God. And, further, I have added that the Catholic doctrine presupposes what in our technical language we call the pre-existence of Him who was born as man into the world, and that I cannot myself conceive how a child born of two parents in what we call the ordinary course of nature could be what I believe our Lord to be the fullest expression of Divine Personality that is possible under the conditions of genuinely human life, the embodiment of God in man. Accordingly, when I reason out the doctrine of the Incarnation, I am, for my part, almost constrained to hold belief in a miraculous birth alongside with my belief in Him of whose Personality I think that doctrine a true interpretation. The one belief is congruous with the other. That is the kind of answer I can give."

With this quite admirable answer, Dr. Bethune-Baker goes on to say he is not satisfied.

"It is, of course, not possible to show that the miraculous Birth was the occasion or original cause of the doctrine; and it is not enough to show that belief in it has been a means of producing belief in the doctrine in later times. If we are to insist on the retention of the belief, we must show how it is vital to the doctrine."

It is true, of course, that it cannot be shown that "the miraculous Birth was the occasion or original cause" of the doctrine of the Incarnation. In its relation to the doctrine of the Incarnation, belief in the Virgin Birth of Our Lord is rather in the nature of effect than original cause or occasion. Christians first believed in the Incarnation, and, as a consequence of this belief, were prepared to accept the fact of the Virgin Birth. As soon as the doctrine of the Incarnation was reasoned out it was necessary to provide an answer to the question "How was the Incarnation effected?" In the absence of a trustworthy tradition, the Church might have been obliged to answer that she did not know. In fact, she has given the answer embodied in the earliest forms of her baptismal Creed, and confirmed by a tradition of facts, which has every appearance of being primitive and trust worthy, that "Jesus Christ was conceived by the Holy Spirit from the Virgin Mary." The only alternative to acceptance of this tradition of facts is to suppose that Jesus was the son, by natural generation, of Joseph and Mary. But such a view, on Dr. Bethune-Baker's own showing, is incompatible with the Catholic doctrine of Our Lord's Person. The connection, then, between the Catholic doctrine of the Incarnation and the fact of Our Lord's Virgin Birth is a vital one. The doctrinal value of the Virgin Birth certainly depends on the Incarnation. And the Church has always believed, ever since the time when she formulated her Creed, that the reality of the Incarnation is safeguarded by belief in the Virgin Birth as a fact.

It is true that in the Apostolic age the doctrine of Christ's Person had not been fully thought out. To work out its implications time and experience were required. But it is fairly clear that the divinely guided instinct of the Church, at a comparatively early stage in the development of doctrine, realized the doctrinal significance of the Virgin Birth. Otherwise, how are we to explain the presence of the clause asserting it in the earliest forms of the baptismal Creed? Indeed, there, as Dr. Bethune Baker is careful to point out, it symbolizes the whole doctrine of the Incarnation. Are we, then, justified in denuding it of historical significance as an assertion of fact, and regarding it as symbolical of the Incarnation generally? In other words, ought those who cannot accept the Virgin Birth as a fact, but yet believe in the Incarnation, to be encouraged to recite the clause in public worship as an expression of belief in the Incarnation generally? For this position, Dr. Bethune Baker puts in a plea, and a teacher whom we all revere, Dr. Sanday, claims that it is legitimate to interpret the clause of the Creed in a symbolical way. He says ---

"In regard to the Birth of our Lord, I would say that I believe most emphatically in his supernatural Birth; but I cannot so easily bring myself to think that His Birth was (as I should regard it) unnatural. This is just a case where I think that the Gospels use symbolical language. I can endorse entirely the substantial meaning of that verse of St. Luke (i. 35) The Holy Ghost shall come upon thee, and the power of the Most High shall overshadow thee where fore also that which is to be born shall be called holy, the Son of God. This is deeply metaphorical and symbolical, and carries us into regions where thought is baffled. I do not doubt that the Birth of our Lord was sanctified in every physical respect in the most perfect manner conceivable. The coming of the Only Begotten into the world could not but be attended by every circumstance of holiness. Whatever the Virgin Birth can spiritually mean for us is guar anteed by the fact that the Holy Babe was Divine. Is it not enough to affirm this with all our heart, and soul, and be silent as to anything beyond?"

This position, it seems to us, amounts to a surrender of the Gospel account of Our Lord s Birth as history; the accounts are either not intended by their writers to be taken literally or are legendary creations. Neither of these views is without grave difficulties, which need not further be discussed here. It is clear that the Church cannot adopt such a position. She cannot surrender what she has regarded, ever since she received it on what seemed to be the highest authority, as a statement of fact defining the method of the Incarnation. The assertion of the fact, apart from an antecedent belief in the reality of the Incarnation, would be of no doctrinal value whatever. But the Church has always believed that this clause of her creed, asserting the fact, safeguards the main doctrine. How can she possibly abandon this position without endangering the doctrine of the Incarnation itself? Neither on historical nor doctrinal grounds, it seems to us, would she be justified in doing so.

It is no doubt possible for individual believers, who have lived for a long time in an atmosphere of belief which has been created by age-long teaching of the full Catholic doctrine, to rest in a position which asserts the reality of the Incarnation apart from the Virgin Birth. But for the Church to adopt such a position authoritatively would surely be disastrous. Sooner or later, the results would inevitably work themselves out in a "reduced" Christology, and a "reduced" Christianity.

Printed in Great Britain
by Amazon

10160876R00058